# THE NEXT CENTURY

ALSO BY NUALA BECK

*Shifting Gears:*
*Thriving in the New Economy*

*Excelerate:*
*Growing in the New Economy*

# THE NEXT CENTURY

## WHY CANADA WINS

### NUALA BECK

HarperCollins*Publishers*Ltd

First edition

Canadian Cataloguing in Publication Data

Beck, Nuala, 1951–
The next century : why Canada wins

ISBN 0-00-255742-8 (bound)
ISBN 0-00-638527-3 (pbk.)

1. Economic forecasting — Canada.
2. Canada — Economic conditions — 1991–   .
I. Title.

HC115.B424 1998    330.871'01'12    C98-930610-0

98 99 00 01 02 03 04 HC 10 9 8 7 6 5 4 3 2 1

Printed and bound in the United States

*For My Dearest Dad*

William J. Broughal
April 1918 – September 1997

And for my wonderful Mom and sister, Liz,
who miss him as much as I do.

# CONTENTS

# TABLES AND CHARTS

# ACKNOWLEDGMENTS

*The Next Century* has its origin in three research projects that began as corporate and government client studies. Two years ago it was heresy to describe Asia's growth markets as a 'has been' trend, and it was equally inconceivable to many that the U.S. dollar was poised to become the strongest currency on the planet. But as our clients know, a disciplined approach to research affords few surprises; it allows us to see the future coming for miles, especially with access to the extraordinary talents of such a fine research team.

Anne-Marie Richter has been my partner and my closest, dearest friend for more years than either we (or our hairdressers) can remember. She occupies the corner office now and runs Nuala Beck & Associates Inc. with exceptional efficiency and a caring heart. I could not imagine my life without her. She wouldn't let me! When she is not keeping me and our firm organized and on track, she is working long hours as the firm's ultimate research whiz, keeping all projects ahead of schedule, and ensuring that my hopes and dreams come true. I couldn't ask for more.

Together with dear friends Joseph Connolly, Eddy Eng and

Melanie Patterson, these special people in my life have made consulting and research efficient and fun. Melanie plays a very special role in all our lives with her devilish sense of fun. I find myself looking forward to birthdays even more than when I was a kid! But she is especially cherished for her kind and generous spirit. Not a day goes by when I don't thank my lucky stars for her patience, warmth and friendship.

Speaking of fine teams, none in the Canadian publishing industry can match the depth and talent at HarperCollins Publishers Ltd. I have enjoyed working with Iris Tupholme, Tom Best, Judy Brunsek and Jan Becker for almost a decade. Their sincerity, professionalism, enthusiasm and commitment are matched by their capacity for kindness and understanding. I sincerely hope that I will have the pleasure of working with these wondered people for many, many, more years, as well as with Nicole Langlois, Sue Thomas and Neil Erickson who, incidentally, have convinced me that an entire manuscript can be crafted effortlessly into a book, within a matter of days!

Now that I again have my weekends free, I am looking forward to special dinners with our closest family and friends at my haven and favourite restaurant, Michael's Back Door, in Mississauga. My husband and I especially enjoy our pleasant chats with good friends Onofrio and Michael.

A balanced life is a good life. I really do believe that, and I am deeply indebted to the family, friends, colleagues and clients who have encouraged me to do what I love best. The chief architects of my happy life are, of course, my husband Frank, our dear Liam, and my partner Anne-Marie. I could never imagine a life without the special magic they weave each day.

Nuala Beck
Toronto, Canada
September 1998

# INTRODUCTION

When the United Nations announced yet again that Canada was the number one country in the world in which to live, like most Canadians, I thought it was a typo.

Surely, they couldn't mean *us*.

We had to be number 11, well behind the countries that count, like Japan Inc., or the Swedes, who stand tall behind all things anti-whatever.

What if Canada's naysayers were right about this country and its hopelessly incompetent institutions? Faced with the tainted-blood scandal, incessant constitutional bickering, mayhem in the military, and the shocking weakness of the Canadian "dollarette" … maybe the bevy of UN economists and their commentators had really meant to say that Canada was number 111.

When Olympic sprinter Donovan Bailey beat the petulant Michael Johnson and became the acknowledged fastest man in the world a second time over, he instinctively draped himself in the Canadian flag, and raced around the track to share his moment of victory with his fellow Canadians, who roared their

1

approval from the stands. The look of confidence and victory on his face was there for the whole world to see. After five consecutive years of international recognition and honour for Canada as the number-one country in the world in which to live, you would think that this country could throw itself a decent street party.

As I pored over the low-key media coverage, I was perplexed by the dearth of cover stories, news specials, and hour-long documentaries celebrating what should have been the story of the century.

Our nation had transformed itself from an economic and financial backwater into the envy of the world. Even an ideologically tainted mini-series would have been a welcome respite from the silence of Concerned Canadians. At the very least, they could have pointed out that Canada remained stagnant at number one, unlike other countries that show improvement over time. God help us all if Canada should slip a notch or two in the UN rankings!

On the other hand, Canadians might be hard-pressed to think of any reason to celebrate as we watch the global economy convulse and once-mighty financial markets around the world vaporize. Moreover, we have just come through the most harrowing time of technological change, job losses, declining incomes, and tax increases in the 1990s that we can remember.

But things do have a habit of changing. Especially when we least expect them to.


As we stand on the threshold of the next century, North America is in the take-off stage, to the greatest era of growth and prosperity the world has seen.

Meanwhile, the rise of the knowledge economy has set in motion the decline of globalization as we know it.

The twenty-first century paradox between the explosion of the Internet and the rise of the knowledge economy fostering the decline of today's global economy has set North America on a remarkably different growth path.

In a stunning twist of history, the emergence of a knowledge economy has altered far more than the nature of work or the fate of companies. It has altered the fate of nations and life as we know it.

As we race towards a future in which so many of the old rules no longer apply, North America is poised to dominate the first half of the next century. Forget Europe, forget Japan, forget China and the Asian Tigers.

Why?

Because the United States has emerged as the indisputable growth leader for the next century.

More than simple optimism, this conclusion is based on hard data. It's based on detailed research. And the conclusions reached in Chapter 3 are undeniable.

Canada already enjoys a formidable lead in the knowledge economy. In terms of its proportion of knowledge workers to the total size of its labour force, Canada already ranks head and shoulders above Japan, the United States, Switzerland, and many, many others. And that's only the first surprise ... of many.

Having survived the Nasty Nineties, we Canadians should be used to surprises. Not long ago, words and phrases such as "downsizing," "life-long learning," "knowledge worker," "information technology," and "the World Wide Web" belonged in the exotic vocabularies of the few. Now they are part and parcel of all our daily lives.

Five powerful trends are sweeping us into the twenty-first century. This book describes these trends, using the new terms and phrases that will become commonplace as the twenty-first century unfolds.

# 1. The Decline of Globalization, As We Know It

The collapse of Asia Pacific, the deep systemic restructuring Japan faces, the economic and political turmoil in the former Soviet Union, South America's fragile grip on economic stability, and the possibility that France, Italy, and Germany could be the world's next financial "surprises" diminish the attractiveness of globalization in a very fundamental way.

Rather than Canadian companies' and mutual fund managers' continuing to pour billions into the global marketplace, they are about to swing their management, marketing, financial, and investment energies 180 degrees, back to North America as never before. Why? Because investment *return-to-risk* profiles (provided in Chapter 3) demand nothing less into the twenty-first century. Although the decline of globalization as we know it has already created immense financial market instability the world over, as markets attempt to sort through the rubble, Canada and the United States are well positioned to thrive in the global vacuum that lies ahead.

# 2. The Growth Surprise

The fallout from international economic turmoil has collapsed the commodity prices on which Canada's resource sector and their suppliers depend. But the "resource recession" will not last forever. Nor will the weakness in the Canadian dollar. Companies that move swiftly to expand their exports to the United States are the ones about to strike it richer than they've dared to dream.

Canada's trading patterns will respond over time to the new conditions. As they do we'll become very familiar with the word "prosperity." In North America 38 industries (15 of them in Canada) are growing faster than what were once the fastest growing economies on earth. The mantra of globalization is already beginning to give way to a remarkably different world economy centred on North America.

## 3. Why Canada Wins

The knowledge economy of the twenty-first century — what I call the New Economy® — is also changing how countries compete with one another and what factors give them a competitive edge. New and powerful advantages in the knowledge economy are displacing the old ones of low wages, abundant natural resources, and access to well-maintained transportation networks:

- Flexibility and transparency: Is it mere coincidence that countries with the highest knowledge ratios have the lowest levels of corruption and those with the lowest knowledge ratios have the highest levels of corruption? Hardly. Canada's low levels of business corruption, which give rise to transparency in business dealings, give us a strong boost in the knowledge economy. In contrast, comparative inflexibility and lack of transparency in Asia, Japan, and Russia, and the protection of old and deeply vested interests in France, Italy, and Germany will shake the foundations of globalization more than the First World War did the old imperial order and balance of power in Europe.
- The electronic immigrant of the twenty-first century: The quest for human capital is changing as highly educated "electronic immigrants" live abroad and commute along the information highway. They boost growth and fill job vacancies in North America on-line. There will be one key difference between the immigration we have known historically: the social, medical, and educational costs of these knowledge workers will be shouldered by their countries of residence,

not by Canada. The process of how national wealth is created is about to change.

- English as the language of the Internet: The World Wide Web has already become the primary platform for international information-sharing and networking. It is also rapidly becoming the platform for global electronic commerce. Anyone who can speak it and surf it has a head start over everyone in the world who can't.
- Quality of life: The ability of communities and countries to retain their asset base of knowledge workers, and to compete for more of them will increasingly define the lead economies of the future. Canada's attractiveness as the best country in the world in which to live gives it an enviable advantage.

## 4. The Great Age of Financial Surpluses

As North America enters the great era of financial surpluses we'll also become very familiar with the term "free money." For Canadians in particular, this will come as a special surprise as well as a unique challenge. As far back in history as the building of the great railroads, Canada has been a nation of systemic deficit producers. As Canadians we have never, ever, had enough money to go around. So we've built a system of government that focuses heavily on income redistribution, along with an entire financial system to support the intermediation business. Money has had to be begged and borrowed, either domestically or abroad. But "free money" — that is, money available almost for free to well-managed companies and responsible individuals — will change the role governments play as well as the role of our banks more profoundly than any other development. Government and banks will have to be restructured or replaced entirely.

As we Canadians save furiously for our retirement years, terms such as "shark attack" will replace "bear market." Waiting for the big bear to lumber out of the forest, ready to pounce on the unwary investor, may describe the slower world of commerce we once knew; it doesn't describe the faster, technologically driven world of just-in-time response that engulfs us now. Canadians would be hard-pressed to think of a single industry today that "lumbers."

Be prepared for razor-sharp declines in companies, industries, economies, and the stock market. We are already seeing these in our current financial news. Workers, managers, consumers, and investors will be thankful to escape these shark attacks in the New Economy without losing an arm or a leg.

## 5. KNOWLEDGE MANAGEMENT

New status symbols will replace the old workplace status symbols of a corner office, an expense account, and a company car. Employers will soon find themselves scrambling to keep their cherished knowledge workers happy, in order to keep them, period. "Knowledge management" and new systems to finance the creation of that knowledge will set the stage for a remarkable era of innovation on this continent. The superstars and innovators across a broad range of disciplines — in business, the arts, and the sciences — will make the security of *intellectual property*, its ownership and applications, a priority.

## THE NEXT CHAPTER IN HUMAN CIVILIZATION

As a country, we're not used to thinking about ourselves as winners. Let alone as a nation respected globally for its prosperity and a sharply rising standard of living. But winning means

7

more than simply amassing a quick pile of electronic cash.

Some nations are perfectly content to accumulate wealth — as Singapore does — or to enjoy the fruits and dividends of past economic achievements as an end in itself — think of France. Occasionally, however, a nation emerges with a vision that sweeps the world into a new and better era in human history.

Have we entered just a new economic era or are we on the edge of an entirely new chapter in human civilization?

Beyond commercial success in the knowledge economy and the tremendous profitability that a decade of intense restructuring has virtually assured us, Canada's prosperity in the twenty-first century opens this possibility. Canada's ability to create a broad balance of achievement and the value and respect that we are willing to ascribe to a great range of accomplishments performed to the highest standards — in literature, art, architecture, philosophy, politics, law, medicine, science, and engineering — will set us apart, more than any one nation's success in simply mastering a new economy.

Classical Greece, the Roman Empire, Renaissance Europe: each bequeathed us legacies far greater than new economies. Each was born out of darkness. Each created a particular culture of achievement that nurtured the human spirit. Could we refer to Canada in a thousand years' time in the same breath as these great civilizations?

As Canadians prepare to take their place as winners in the knowledge economy, we should try to preserve those qualities that make us who we are as a people. We are humane and hardworking. We possess a quiet, extraordinary confidence alongside a healthy humility and collective caring and respect for one another.

The choices we face, the debates that lie ahead, are daunting, rousing, exhilarating, in equal measure. Just like the next century, the Canadian century.

# ARE YOU READY FOR THE NEXT CENTURY?

Take this short quiz to discover why Canada wins.

**1. Despite its current problems, Japan still enjoys an enviable lead in today's high knowledge economy. True or false?**

False. With 32.8 knowledge workers per 100 employees, Canada enjoys a staggering lead over Japan's 16.1 knowledge workers per 100 employees.

**2. Canada leads the United States with an impressively high number of knowledge workers per 100 employees. True or false?**

True. With 32.8 knowledge workers per 100 employees, Canada is ahead of the United States with its 31.9 knowledge workers per 100 employees.

**3. America's economic growth rate is rising structurally and the country is poised to dominate the first half of the twenty-first century. True or false?**

True. In Chapter 4 you'll read about the industries that are growing faster than what were once the fastest growing economies on earth.

**4. Globalization has had its day. It's a safer bet for Canadian companies to concentrate on the opportunities for growth in the United States. True or false?**

True. A blind faith in globalization will destroy many of Canada's mightiest corporations. Why? Because the return versus the risk

9

of global investment into the next century has changed swiftly and decisively.

**5. As one of the world's fastest growing economies, Hong Kong continues to be a force to be reckoned with in the information age. True or false?**

False. Microsoft, just one American company, has a market capitalization of more than $250 billion, making it larger than the entire gross domestic product of Hong Kong.

**6. Canada is well positioned for the information age of the twenty-first century. True or false?**

True. With 55.0 telephone lines per 100 inhabitants, Canada has greater access to information than India, Indonesia, the Philippines, Thailand, Malaysia, and China combined.

**7. Germany and France will power a "New Europe" and become an important growth engine in the wake of Asia's economic collapse. True or false?**

False. The New Europe is being led by the U.K. and is powered by a surprising group of dark horses. The Netherlands, Ireland, Finland, and Denmark are the real forces to be reckoned with.

**8. After decades of deficit spending, the United States still relies on foreign capital to keep interest rates low. True or false?**

False — no longer the case! The American economy began generating extraordinary financial surpluses in the 1990s. In the first quarter of 1998, the United States generated US$57.8 billion more in national capital than it could immediately use.

**9. As the twenty-first century approaches, interest rates will fall further and free money will become available to the well-managed company and responsible individual. True or false?**

True. *The Next Century* explains the new rules for finance as we race towards the future and why many of the old rules no longer apply.

**10. Job security will continue to be a major issue for Canadians well into the next century. True or false?**

False. This book describes the lengths your company will soon be willing to go to keep its knowledge workers contented. Know what new perks are replacing the old ones and how your organization's learning budget can be invested to effectively manage your knowledge workers, your greatest asset.

# 1

# THE STORY
# OF THE CENTURY

What is Canada's most strategic asset? The abundance of our natural resources? The richness of our prairies and farmlands? Or our vast coastlines, which provide access to three of the world's great oceans?

None of the above. It's knowledge.

Unlike the wealth derived from oceans, minerals, forests, and farmlands, today's knowledge economy doesn't depend on luck, fate, or natural endowments. Knowledge — our society's ability to develop new know-how and create new products, new processes, and new markets through applying that knowledge — is based solely on our own ability, drive, and determination as individuals and as a country.

The knowledge economy has changed how wealth is created and what it is created from. It has profoundly changed the future of Canada and of the United States, Japan, Mexico, and the other countries and continents that we trade with, and invest in.

As we race towards a future in which so many of the old rules no longer apply, the company, the industry, and the country with the most productive knowledge workers will win. Smart companies, organizations, and communities will outperform and create wealth and opportunity. The others will fall by the wayside.

For Canadians, the choice is simple: *Ignore the emerging trends and be left behind, or capitalize on those trends as never before.*

# Canada's Lead in the Knowledge Economy

My consulting firm set out to measure the knowledge base of 40 countries around the world. Through this eye-opening study we now know with certainty that Canada and the United States are out in front in the new knowledge economy, among the leaders of the pack.

Hard data from the International Labour Organization in Geneva, Switzerland, support this claim. With 32.8 knowledge workers per 100 employees — the standard measurement which my firm developed of a nation's knowledge base — Canada leads the United States with its 31.9 knowledge workers per 100 employees. Canada also enjoys nearly a two-fold lead over Japan, where knowledge workers account for 16.1 percent of that nation's workforce.

Knowledge workers, the people who are paid to *think*, and not just *do,* include professionals such as doctors, professors, and accountants; the ranks of senior management; and, most important, the engineering, technical, and scientific workers who form the backbone of the knowledge economy.

The table on page 14 summarizes our research into international knowledge ratios. The results invite interesting comparisons and observations.

13

# How the Global Knowledge Base Compares
## An International Analysis

| | COUNTRY | 1996 | 1993 | 1990 |
|---|---|---|---|---|
| | 1. Netherlands | 44.1 | 28.7 | 28.1 |
| H | 2. Singapore | 37.3 | 30.7 | 26.3 (1991) |
| I | 3. Germany | 37.2 | 34.4 | — |
| G | 4. Denmark | 36.7* | 30.0 | 28.1 |
| H | 5. New Zealand | 36.2* | 36.8 | 24.4 |
| | 6. United Kingdom | 35.9* | 34.6 | — |
| K | 7. Sweden | 35.6 (1995) | 34.2 | 32.0 |
| N | 8. Iceland | 35.0 | 33.2 | 31.4 (1991) |
| O | 9. Czech Republic | 34.0 | 32.2 | — |
| W | 10. Finland | 33.3 | 31.3 | 28.6 |
| L | **11. Canada** | **32.8** | **32.5** | **30.2** |
| E | 12. Norway | 32.4 (1995) | 32.4 | 30.0 |
| D | **13. United States** | **31.9** | **30.2** | **29.0** |
| G | 14. Ireland | 31.2 | 29.8 | 27.9 |
| E | 15. Israel | 30.9* | 29.9 | 30.1 |
| | 16. Hungary | 29.4 | — | — |
| | 17. Austria | 28.9 (1995)* | 21.6 | 20.8 |
| | 18. Hong Kong | 28.5* | 14.3 | 12.4 |
| | 19. Spain | 27.5* | 14.4 | 12.8 |
| | 20. Greece | 27.0 (1995)* | 25.7 | 14.3 |
| | 21. Poland | 26.7 | — | — |
| | 22. Belgium | — | 26.3 (1992) | 25.4 |
| | 23. Portugal | 25.1* | 26.9 | 11.0 |
| | 24. Australia | — | 24.9 | 23.7 |
| | 25. Switzerland | 19.8 | 20.0 | 15.9 (1991) |
| | 26. Egypt | 17.8 (1995) | 17.6 | 14.9 |
| | 27. Korea | 17.0* | 15.1 | 8.7 |
| | **28. Japan** | **16.1** | **15.7** | **14.9** |
| | 29. Venezuela | 15.7 (1995) | 16.2 | 16.6 |
| | 30. Mexico | 15.5* | 10.9 | 11.5 (1991) |
| | 31. Malaysia | 13.5 | 11.6 | 9.9 |
| | 32. Chile | 12.0 | 12.0 | 12.3 |
| | 33. Italy | 10.6 (1995) | — | — |
| | 34. Turkey | 7.8 | 8.5 | 8.2 |
| | 35. Philippines | 7.6 | 7.1 | 7.4 |
| | 36. Brazil | 7.5 (1995) | 7.3 | 7.5 |
| | 37. Thailand | — | — | 4.8 |
| | 38. Pakistan | 6.0 (1995) | 6.0 | 4.5 |
| | 39. France | — | — | — |

Sources: ILO and Nuala Beck & Associates Inc. The *Yearbook of Labour Statistics* is an annual publication of the International Labour Office, prepared by the Bureau of Statistics. The publication covers labour statistics for more than 180 countries, areas, and territories. Occupational data are classified according to the International Standard Classification of Occupations (ISCO), 1988. An asterisk (*) denotes that previous year's data is based on ISCO classifications for 1968. A dash (—) indicates that data was not available.

It's not unreasonable to ask why Canada leads or why a country such as Japan, with 16.1 knowledge workers per 100 employees, lags so far behind North America.

A story I heard about Japanese workers may help explain the gap. A 40-something Japanese middle manager — a salaryman, as he's called — became visibly distraught when the vice-president of his company informed him that he would be honoured with a window office that afforded him a nice view. When I asked why a window office was considered so godawful, I was told it was a sign that the organization no longer needed him; he realized he would be left to sit by that window until his days in the workforce were over.

In Canada we used to call that "being put out to pasture." Canadian companies know that their livelihoods depend on being innovative, being able to respond quickly to change. Our secret weapon? Flexibility. We're the flexible, adaptable economy in the knowledge age. Japan isn't.

North America's widely used separation packages and early-retirement programs have given our economy the flexibility to change with the times. These tools have allowed organizations to restructure themselves and adapt quickly to new technologies and product lines — in short, to adopt the new business model. Big, bloated, slow-moving companies that require their employees to spend endless hours shuffling paper and projects to and fro are the natural-born killers of innovation, the essential ingredient of a knowledge economy. As the world's slowest growing industrialized economy, Japan is learning this lesson the hard way.

Japanese companies have been reluctant to restructure along new lines and have zealously protected many notoriously inefficient domestic industries, such as agriculture and banking. Japan still prohibits importing any foreign rice, to protect its small farmers, even though Japanese rice therefore costs six times the world price for it! This xenophobic attitude is taking a toll that

**15**

shows up clearly in its knowledge ratio, which has sunk to 28th place in our international rankings.

As the elderly director of one of Japan's great manufacturing empires told me quietly, "It is a matter of great shame for Japanese companies to admit that they made a mistake and no longer have a job for every worker."

After five years of near-zero growth and currently in the throes of a deep recession, Japanese companies would be desperate, you would think, for a new approach. Surely they would be willing to set aside some of the traditions that actually threaten their economic survival. But evidence of restructuring remains spotty.

One horror story went the rounds in Tokyo about a hidebound company's managers who couldn't bring themselves to tell an employee that they no longer had any work for him. Instead of offering him a dignified termination and a decent separation package, they assigned him the task of writing an essay every two weeks, entitled "My Second Life." To find fresh ideas for his ongoing corporate assignment, he studied a book about the lives of insects each week. Can you imagine that happening in a Canadian company today?

Unlike Japan, Singapore boasts a dynamic economy with important strategic advantages. That country earns our admiration for having the highest knowledge base in the Pacific Rim. With its open-for-business attitude, Singapore has consolidated its importance as a centre of finance and technology in Asia.

Meanwhile, by 1996, the latest year for which data are available Hong Kong's knowledge ratio continued to rise, if only to 28.5. At first glance, this fact puzzled me.

But with thousands of Hong Kong's best and brightest seeking more stable political futures elsewhere in advance of China's takeover of the former British colony, emigration has drained much of the knowledge base of the country. Little wonder Canada has welcomed its influx of immigrants from Hong Kong.

Knowledge workers are welcome anywhere. (As a side note, it will be interesting to watch developments in Hong Kong and whether its knowledge ratio rises, falls, or stagnates under Chinese rule in the years to come.)

Other observations about Canada's standing in the world of knowledge are equally fascinating: at 32.8, Canada's knowledge ratio is more than double that of Mexico, with 15.5. In fact, we enjoy the highest knowledge ratio in the Americas.

On the other side of the Atlantic, who would have guessed that the Republic of Ireland takes an impressive lead in the knowledge economy? With 31.2 knowledge workers per 100 employees, it ranks ahead of both Japan and Hong Kong. It is a major player in pharmaceuticals and electronics. It is also one of the world's leading exporters of software, thanks to its high-knowledge base and open-for-business attitude.

Ireland has made enviable strides in educating its knowledge workers for the next millennium and continues to boost spending on education. This increased spending — a 40 percent increase in the last five years alone — may seem inconceivable to beleaguered Canadians. By 1997 Ireland had abolished all tuition fees at universities and colleges, and the country's farsighted government is working rapidly to abolish tuition fees for part-time students as well. The country has embraced the concept of lifelong learning and accordingly has been rewarded with an economy that has grown by 62 percent in the last five years!

Along with other Nordic European countries, Ireland could become a formidable competitive force in the twenty-first century along with Denmark at 36.7, Sweden at 35.6, Iceland with 35.0, Finland with 33.3, and Norway with 32.4 knowledge workers per 100 people employed. All of these nations are worth watching carefully. They represent the greatest challenge for the future. Naturally, they also represent extremely attractive export markets for Canadian high-knowledge companies.

## Nordic Europe's Knowledge Edge

| COUNTRY | 1996 | 1990 |
|---------|------|------|
| Denmark | 36.7 | 28.1 |
| Sweden | 35.6 (1995) | 32.0 |
| Iceland | 35.0 | 31.4 (1991) |
| Finland | 33.3 | 28.6 |
| Norway | 32.4 (1995) | 30.0 |
| Ireland | 31.2 | 27.9 |

Source: ILO and Nuala Beck & Associates Inc.

Unlike Ireland, not all countries are headed in the right direction. Venezuela's knowledge ratio has actually fallen, for instance, and the knowledge ratios of countries like Chile and the Philippines have stagnated in the past five years. Pakistan, the Philippines, Brazil, and Turkey cluster together at the very bottom of the knowledge rankings.

It's pure nonsense to think that low-knowledge countries in either Latin America or Asia pose the biggest threats to Canada's competitive advantage in the twenty-first century. These other countries are great with the busy-finger work; in terms of high knowledge, however, they barely count.

# Canada's Knowledge Elite

To understand the dynamics of global growth and the challenge a knowledge economy presents for Canada, we need to familiarize ourselves with this knowledge base that underpins our future. The question of how to define the knowledge worker of the information age was among the first challenges we faced at my consulting firm. Many research groups have tried repeatedly to link knowledge to educational attainment and to quantify knowledge workers by the number of college graduates or PhDs coming out of a country's educational system. It didn't take us long to recognize that defining these workers according to the work they actually *perform* makes far more sense.

Few would argue that Bill Gates, founder of Microsoft, should be disqualified as a knowledge worker because he never earned a college or university degree. Matthew Barrett, Bank of Montreal's CEO, never completed one either, though both of these leaders have received many honorary degrees in the course of their business careers.

The PhD driving a taxi may have impressive academic credentials but isn't employing that special knowledge on the job. Therefore this person, we decided, should not be counted as one of our knowledge workers. It also seems reasonable to assume that the hiring process weeds out those applicants who do not have the skills or knowledge necessary to carry out a "knowledge" job.

Occupation, then, and not educational attainment, is more useful as a criterion used to define knowledge workers. Many production workers have been retrained as technical workers through a broad range of accredited certificate, diploma, and degree programs, or on-the-job training, too. A good number of them have gone on to become knowledge workers in the New Economy.

Accordingly, Nuala Beck & Associates Inc. defines knowledge workers as those employed in the following occupational categories:

1. **Professionals**, such as engineers, lawyers, doctors, professors, accountants, and actuaries. These and many other professional service providers exemplify specialized knowledge and they have the academic credentials, often required by law, to back it up. The demand for these skills and knowledge has generated dramatic growth in professional services. Reflecting real growth of 40 percent between 1992 and 1997, professional services have flourished in Canada and elsewhere.

**19**

2. **The very senior ranks of management.** These are the business leaders of the organization who are paid to think. Most CEOs have university degrees; many have more than one. These leaders often acquire the knowledge they need in diverse, even unconventional, ways, some, like Matthew Barrett and Bill Gates, proudly call themselves self-made men.

3. **Engineering, scientific, and technical workers.** This category is not strictly related to individual levels of educational attainment, either. It is closely associated with the specialized skills and knowledge base each person develops on his or her own, outside formal learning.

We applied these definitions to monthly employment data from the Bureau of Labor Statistics to establish a benchmark of U.S. data for nearly 300 industries. Then we extended our analysis by applying those ratios to the Canadian employment data that Statistics Canada publishes every month for those same industries and for each of our provinces.

We spent months studying countless trends across industries and provinces. Each new trend we uncovered proved more interesting than the one before it.

However, when the Quebec data started rolling in, we couldn't believe our eyes. Quebec accounted for 90 percent of Canada's high-knowledge professional service sector job losses in the last five years. We couldn't resist taking a closer look, and digging deeper to find the reasons why.

## The Two Solitudes

The term "two solitudes" is most often used to describe Canada's internal political and cultural polarization. It might just as well describe the rapid polarization within the knowledge economy, between Quebec and the rest of Canada. The chart on the following page shows just how far Quebec lags behind.

What I found particularly baffling is that Quebec enjoyed a wholesome lead in the knowledge economy of the 1980s and early 1990s: the creation of CEGEPs (Collèges d'Enseignement Général et Professionnel, the equivalent of community colleges in the rest of Canada) across the province and Quebec's emphasis on education created a vital pool of knowledge workers; the Quebec Stock Savings Plan assured young technology companies of readier access to capital than many of their counterparts enjoyed in the rest of the country.

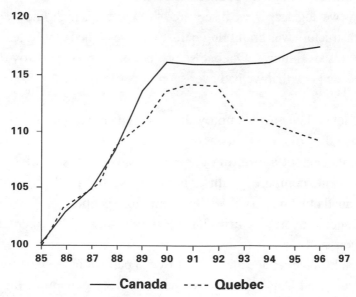

## How Quebec Compares to Canada:
## High-Knowledge Employment Trends
### (1985 = 100)

Sources: Statistics Canada, Nuala Beck & Associates Inc.

For a while these initiatives paid off. Between 1985 and 1995, high-knowledge industries created more than twice as many new jobs as moderate- and low-knowledge industries in Quebec combined, net of job losses. And by the mid 1990s, Quebec had a higher proportion of people employed in high-knowledge industries than the rest of Canada. Today, more Quebecers are employed in the software and systems industry than in the province's mining and forestry industries combined. According to Price Waterhouse, Montreal ranks only slightly behind San Francisco in information technology. Quebec's telecos — telecommunications companies — employ more people than the residential construction industry does, while broadcasting employs more than the beverage, wine, and beer industries combined. On the surface, then, Quebec's high-technology sectors looked as vibrant as ever in 1996. So what accounted for the drastic decline in Quebec's high-knowledge sector?

As we dug deeper, we discovered that Quebec's high-knowledge infrastructure was crumbling before our eyes. The layoff rates and job losses among Quebec's professional service providers exceeded any that we had ever seen.

- Quebec law firms employ 26.6 percent fewer people now than they did five years ago.
- Management consulting companies saw job losses of 10.2 percent, compared with a booming sector in the rest of Canada that has hired 18.7 percent more people.
- Quebec advertising firms have lost more than 13.9 percent of their staff.
- Banks have reduced their staff by 5.5 percent in the past five years, and Caisse populaires have cut 18.1 percent of their employees. Trust company employment fell by 49.3 percent.
- Investment intermediaries, such as brokers and financial planners, employ 29.9 percent fewer Quebecers now than they did

five years ago. (The real challenge remains: determining whether these financial wizards rank among Quebec's knowledge elite!)

In 1996, Quebec's investment sector dropped out of the high-knowledge category as a whole as knowledge workers declined as a percentage of the total number of people employed in that industry. By 1997, Quebec's investment industry had moved back into the high-knowledge category — barely.

Now, I'll be the first to admit you don't need to be a knowledge worker to make money when the stock market is on a roll, when almost anything an investor touches turns to gold. Only when a portfolio manager friend of mine, whom I'll call Ed, told me about his trip to Quebec City did I appreciate how poorly equipped many members of Quebec's financial community are to meet the demands of this fast-paced knowledge economy.

During RRSP season, Ed was scheduled to speak to brokers and financial planners at the elegant Château Frontenac in Quebec City one frigid February morning. Nothing looked particularly amiss. The usual assortment of well-dressed guys paraded through the lobby, morning newspapers in hand, ready to hear all about the latest mutual fund that had just come down from on high at First Canadian Place on the corner of Bay and King in Toronto.

"As I stood up to address the hundred or so guys in the room, the place started to look like a low-budget version of the United Nations. At first, I couldn't figure out what they were all fiddling with in their seats, until I realized that almost everyone in the room was reaching for earphones. They couldn't understand enough English to follow my presentation!

"Afterwards, I asked our local rep how these financial people could function. 'How do they read the *Wall Street Journal*?' I asked.

" 'They don't,' came the reply.

" 'What about the *Globe and Mail*'s *Report on Business* each morning, or a weekly copy of *Barron's*?' How could these people *operate* without access to market information and timely analysis?"

Most of them, it seemed, simply rely on Quebec-based portfolio managers and analysts to do the reading and analysis for them and pass along what they need to know and tell their clients about *en français*. I think I'd sleep better at night knowing that my financial planner or broker could read a newspaper and make informed decisions for herself.

## Why Has Quebec's High-Knowledge Sector Collapsed?

The collapse of Quebec's high-knowledge sector could not be explained away by industry restructuring or restrictive language laws or poor economic performance or even by the departure of anglophones and ethnics from Quebec — the largest migration in North American history!

By separating Quebec's high-knowledge sector into its three component parts as follows, we found answers to questions that we had never expected to ask.

1. Knowledge-based business — pharmaceuticals, telecommunications, information technology, aerospace. Think of this group as the formula race car drivers in Quebec's knowledge economy.

2. Professional services — banking, accounting and legal services, management consulting. These serve as the support vital to knowledge-based businesses that drive today's knowledge economy. Think of this group as the highly skilled mechanics who keep the race cars delivering peak performance.

3. Public sector infrastructure — government, education, social, and health services. Think of this group as the race organizers and officials who ensure a world-class Grand Prix event.

Between 1991 and 1996 Quebec's private sector infrastructure has declined 13.5 percent based on the number of people it now employs. With a drop of 13.5 percent in the number of professional service providers, the carnage has been greatest among professional services — the super-skilled mechanics of the knowledge age. By comparison, Quebec's public service has done well for itself; it employs only 2.5 percent fewer people than it did five years ago. Quebec's knowledge-based business sector has actually increased the number of people it employs.

By process of elimination, the problem was easy to spot. Quebec's professional service sector was in free fall. (The decline is shown vividly in the graph on page 28.)

It would be foolish to think that Quebec's high-knowledge businesses can maintain their competitive edge without just-in-time access to a large and varied pool of expertise in banking, law, finance, accounting, and the many other professional services that provide the vital infrastructure of the knowledge economy.

# Pierre's Story

Pierre's story is not an uncommon one in Quebec. In 1996, at 46 years of age, Pierre found that the law firm he was a partner of closed its doors on fashionable Sherbrooke Street in downtown Montreal.

"If we were a small pulp mill on the outskirts of Rimouski, the place would be crawling with reporters and TV cameras." The anger and frustration were clear in Pierre's voice. "A couple of guys with a grade eight education lose their jobs and Radio Canada does a week-long call-in program about how people suffer when technology changes. But for a guy like me who has lost his only profession, no one gives a damn.

"My biggest clients were in industries that no longer exist. How many retraining programs do you think I could apply for? What do you think are my chances of ever working again? I'll tell you. The Leafs have a better chance of winning a Stanley Cup than I do of ever working again. I can't go to Toronto or anywhere else, for that matter. No one else uses Quebec's Civil Code." (Every other legal jurisdiction in Canada follows British common law, not the French Civil Code.)

Along with Pierre, there are 27,000 professional-service company employees, partners, and owners whose lives have been derailed since 1991 and who suffer in silence, far away from the cameras and microphones that document a changing Quebec.

## The Rise and Fall of Quebec's Knowledge Economy

The steady decline in Quebec's high-knowledge employment levels since 1991, shown in the table on page 27, suggests that no one event is responsible for this decline. What is more likely is that many ingredients have combined to erode Quebec's high-knowledge health:

• Montreal's appeal as a head office location has declined.

# Growth of High-Knowledge Employment
## for Canada and Quebec
## 1983–1996

| YEAR | CANADA | QUEBEC |
|------|--------|--------|
| | NUMBER OF PERSONS EMPLOYED | |
| 1983 | 2,951,388 | 777,250 |
| 1984 | 3,000,297 | 791,983 |
| 1985 | 3,085,608 | 813,142 |
| 1986 | 3,167,186 | 840,036 |
| 1987 | 3,255,944 | 855,455 |
| 1988 | 3,351,645 | 883,896 |
| 1989 | 3,482,254 | 899,718 |
| 1990 | 3,584,187 | 923,016 |
| 1991 | 3,585,605 | 928,861 |
| 1992 | 3,571,069 | 927,998 |
| 1993 | 3,569,287 | 903,972 |
| 1994 | 3,573,402 | 902,378 |
| 1995 | 3,602,360 | 894,642 |
| 1996 | 3,613,608 | 890,394 |
| | GROWTH RATES | |
| 1985–1990 | 16.2% | 13.5% |
| 1990–1995 | 0.5% | -3.1% |
| 1985–1995 | 16.7% | 10.0% |
| 1986–1996 | 14.1% | 6.0% |
| 1995–1996 | 0.3% | -0.5% |

Sources: Statistics Canada, Nuala Beck & Associates Inc.

- Professionals migrate to what they perceive are greater opportunities and a more stable political future outside the province.
- Industry restructurings have centralized professional expertise elsewhere.
- A change in the risk-adjusted returns for professional-service companies have made moving capital to other parts of the world more attractive for these companies, to Brussels or Manchester rather than Montreal.

• As old industries fade and the old client bases shrink, many professionals may find their expertise redundant to a new client base with new needs and interests.

As shown by the graph below, the virtual collapse of Quebec's professional-service sector also raises the alarm that Quebec's knowledge-based businesses will be unable to sustain themselves in Quebec. As these businesses in Quebec grow and their needs expand, increasingly they will be forced to seek elsewhere (in Canada or in the United States) the high-knowledge services absolutely vital to remaining competitive in today's knowledge economy.

## Quebec: Total Professional Service Sector Employment as a % of Total Employment

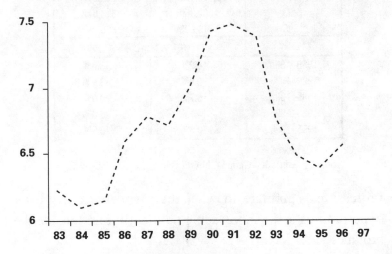

Sources: Statistics Canada, Nuala Beck & Associates Inc.

If legal, banking, accounting, and all the other high-knowledge services that support the growth of knowledge-based businesses are not readily available to high tech companies on a just-in-time basis in Quebec, then those knowledge-based firms will face one of two grim choices:

- Either remain in Quebec and suffer potentially fatal challenges to their competitive advantage and ability to respond rapidly to changes in their markets, or,
- Move to other locations where high-knowledge services are instantly available.

## "Bonjour, y'all"

While Toronto, Ottawa, and Vancouver may come to mind as locations where high-knowledge services are readily available in Canada, Boston, Seattle, and San Francisco, among other U.S. cities, are the really serious contenders. Quebec's trade flows have shifted rapidly from east-west to north-south. By 1997, 82 percent of the exports leaving Quebec were headed for the United States. Our immediate neighbour to the south is in a position to attract high-tech companies with its vast pools of innovation capital. This, coupled with the breadth and scope of top talent available to the highest bidder on a contract basis, may prove too tempting for many Quebec software, information services, and systems companies to resist.

Ultimately, the real risk to Quebec's cultural identity in the twenty-first century may have little to do with its relations with the rest of Canada.

Strong and strengthening trade ties to the United States present the real risk to the province's culture because its high-knowledge companies will find themselves forced to move closer to those high-knowledge accounting, legal, and financial services that sustain their competitive edge.

Quebec's French language and culture could well be assimilated into the American melting pot in the next century, much as francophone Louisiana was absorbed into the mainstream of American culture in the last century. The example of Quebec

29

demonstrates how provinces that were once the leaders can lag
behind in the New Economy, and how whole countries can also
find themselves out of the running as the very nature of competitive advantage is transformed before our eyes.

# 2

# WHY CANADA WINS

## OLD ADVANTAGES AREN'T WORTH THEIR SALT

Long before the modern age of salt-free everything, salt itself was a valuable resource. In ancient and medieval times, access to the mineral was a huge competitive advantage. The power to control a population's salt supply was power over life and death because, as far back as 2700 B.C., salt was the food preservative of choice. Roman soldiers were paid in packets of salt which they used to preserve fish, game, and fowl.

Much of the world's early economic development took place in those countries of warm climates, principally around the Mediterranean Sea, the Black Sea, and the Nile basin, where salt could be produced by evaporating sea water.

Over the course of history battles were fought and revolutions sparked over the supply of this mineral. Those who controlled its distribution possessed tremendous economic and financial power. For example, French kings developed a salt monopoly that favoured the very wealthy and so enraged the citizens of France to the point where a revolution became unavoidable. Those of limited means in France often could not afford this precious mineral and so developed flavourful sauces to mask the taste of rancid meat and rotting fowl. (Hence the development of haute cuisine and such world-famous dishes as coq au vin, boeuf bourguignon, and canard à l'orange.)

Although few countries today would brag that "We're a salt-based economy," Canada and the United States actually control one-third of the world's salt production. The first patent the British Crown ever granted in America gave Samuel Winslow the exclusive right to produce salt for a period of ten years. In today's world, Intel and IBM patents on a new microchip make the evening news reports on new technology and the competitive advantages it confers. When did *The National* last feature Canada's lock grip on the salt market?

What constitutes a competitive advantage, then, can change. New forms of such advantages are popping up all the time, and with greater and greater speed as the twentieth century draws to a close.

Beyond resource riches, countries used to pride themselves on their fine ports. Before the advent of FedEx and container loads of airfreight, a well laid-out port automatically benefited any country that based its economy on trade. The merchants of Venice capitalized on their natural strategic advantages by building an entire city around their canal system. This in turn spawned yet another wealth-creating industry — the gondola business, one of the first great transit systems of Europe.

Today, countries such as Canada, Ireland, and the Netherlands recognize that their knowledge base rather than their historic access to the sea will determine their futures, a point that has often been overlooked by some premiers in Atlantic Canada.

So what if our basic wage rates in Canada are high compared to those of developing economies? As long as we are competitive, innovative, and maintain the finest education system in the world to grow and sustain our knowledge base, when it comes to knowledge work, we can and should let the busy-finger work move elsewhere. That way other nations can benefit from the prosperity that those low-knowledge industries once provided to us before we moved up the knowledge ladder of economic development.

# WINNING IN THE KNOWLEDGE ECONOMY

By the turn of this century, old competitive advantages that used to matter a great deal will have been swept aside as other critical advantages emerge to replace them, dictating a new batch of global economic winners. From salt and resource riches, from low wage rates to good ports, highways, and railroads, old advantages are giving way to whole new sets of economic rules that will dictate who triumphs economically in the next century.

The country with the most productive knowledge workers will thrive. The very basis of comparative advantage upon which growth and prosperity have been based are unfolding at a breathtaking rate. New technologies and new skills open up opportunities to develop new products, new markets, new industries, and for entire countries, to manage powerful new competitive advantages, some unimaginable only a few years ago.

There are many countries contending for domination of the knowledge economy of the twenty-first century. Not every one of them stands to make it into the winner's circle. Some, such as France and Austria in the 1990s, are protecting old industries at the expense of the new advantages by which they could create new wealth.

But what factors are at play? Why does North America have a competitive advantage? Why are Canada and the United States positioned to exercise impressive leadership in the knowledge economy? And why, on the other hand, do many countries, such as Switzerland, already lag so far behind us?

Each era can be defined by its knowledge base and the competitive factors or advantages that underpinned it — from the Industrial Revolution to this century's mass manufacturing age to the new information technology era in which we now find ourselves.

Now for some comparisons. Brazil, with 7.5 knowledge workers per 100 people employed, is firmly entrenched in a commodity-processing economy. Its low proportion of knowledge workers seriously hampers its ability to compete nationally in the high-knowledge economy. And Brazil's economic policy-makers, under great internal pressure to create jobs, will make concerted efforts either to attract foreign investment in low-knowledge industries or to make such industries priorities in their domestic agendas. Brazil needs industries that can employ its available workforce, which is largely unskilled. This knowledge barrier will bar Brazil and countries such as Turkey and Pakistan from competing in this high-knowledge world.

Only if Brazil could raise its knowledge base sharply through massive investments in education could it begin to set its sights on moving into a high-knowledge arena. Ascending the next rung of economic development would move the nation into the world of manufacturing and enable it to challenge countries whose moderately knowledge-intensive industries command that kind of economy.

Malaysia has managed to accomplish just that. Between 1990 and 1996, that country expanded its knowledge base from 9.9 percent to 13.5 percent. It also became an important exporter of light manufacturing and component work. Interestingly, Japan, once the world leader in manufacturing, has failed to advance and therefore keep up. Singapore poses a startling contrast to Japan; the tinier Singapore didn't even exist as a country some 35 years ago. Today its society enjoys the second highest knowledge base in the world, proving dramatically that countries can thrust themselves up the economic development ladder if they set their minds to it. More recently, Ireland and the Netherlands have been catapulted into the winner's circle — the Netherlands ranks as number one, with the highest knowledge base in the world.

Contrast these countries with North America. Canada and the United States have moved at breakneck speed to define and dominate the information age. Clearly we operate in a league of our own now, in terms of potential prosperity and growth.

Over the past decade, Canada has restructured its economy, shifting quickly from its traditional reliance on natural resources to its knowledge resources. Our knowledge ratio of 30.2 percent in 1990 has improved to 32.8 percent for year-end 1996.

Today's widely used measures of competitiveness include:

- Science and technology: These measure whether a country has the technological capacity in place to compete. Countries that admit to having trouble spelling "R & D" obviously score low in this area.
- Management: Well-trained managers are a big feature in the knowledge age when countries try to attract foreign companies or keep the ones they have.
- Government: Just as some companies can't manage their way out of paper bags, so entire countries can face the same problem. A responsive government open to new ideas is a definite plus.
- Infrastructure: First-rate telecommunications are to the New Economy what well-maintained ports were to the old.
- Finance: As always, ready access to domestic capital for financing growth gives any country an edge.
- Education: Ireland has upped the international ante by providing free college and university education. It is only a matter of time until Canada and other countries feel the pressure to keep up.

# Knowledge Ladder of Economic Development* 1997

## 1880–1918

### Commodity-Driven Era

| Knowledge Ratio of Major Industries | |
|---|---|
| Malaysia | 14.7% |
| Chile | 13.5 |
| Italy | 12.0 |
| Turkey | 10.6 |
| Philippines | 7.8 |
| Brazil | 7.6 |
| Pakistan | 7.5 |
| | 6.0 |

## 1918–1981

### Manufacturing-Driven Era

| Knowledge Ratio of Major Industries | |
|---|---|
| Egypt | 18.0% |
| Korea | 17.8 |
| Japan | 17.0 |
| Venezuela | 16.1 |
| Mexico | 15.7 |
| | 15.5 |

## 1981–2035

### Technology-Driven Era

| Knowledge Ratio of Major Industries | |
|---|---|
| Netherlands | 48.9% |
| Singapore | 44.1 |
| Germany | 37.3 |
| Denmark | 37.2 |
| New Zealand | 36.7 |
| United Kingdom | 36.2 |
| Sweden | 35.9 |
| Iceland | 35.6 |
| Czech Republic | 35.0 |
| Finland | 34.0 |
| Canada | 33.3 |
| Norway | 32.8 |
| United States | 32.4 |
| Ireland | 31.9 |
| Israel | 31.2 |
| Hungary | 30.9 |
| Austria | 29.4 |
| Hong Kong | 28.9 |
| Spain | 28.5 |
| Poland | 27.5 |
| Portugal | 26.7 |
| Switzerland | 25.1 |
| | 19.8 |

*Based on 1996 Country Knowledge Ratios

Source: Nuala Beck & Associates Inc.

- Internationalization: Countries that declare themselves open for business stay in business for a long time. In other words, attitude counts.
- Domestic Economy: Well-developed, diversified national economies beat out those that concentrate on one product or resource.
- People: A healthy, educated workforce with a well-developed work ethic and a peaceful and law-abiding society — a big plus for any company anywhere.

# Competitive Advantage in the Knowledge Economy

There's never a shortage of things to do on a free afternoon in New York City. One October day several years ago I took a cab to midtown along the East River instead of enjoying one of my more usual pursuits, like visiting the Met or checking out the sales at Saks.

The two hours that I spent just off the lobby of the United Nations headquarters that afternoon have changed forever the way I see Canada's future and the future of many developing countries. That time sparked the beginning of my major research passion for the next two years and culminated in this book.

I signed up for the tour that takes more than 400,000 tourists and visitors through the building each year. I never made it past the tour guide's opening spiel. Just off the lobby, a few minutes into the tour, I found myself staring up at an enormous map of the world. Dramatically displayed in primary colours were the various populations of the world's nations and world incomes. The bright little dots showed where most of the world's wealthiest and poorest people were spread over the globe.

Why are the most populous areas of the world the poorest? I asked myself. Labour as one of the key factors in production had been drummed into my head since my early days as a young economist. If a large and willing labour force was as vital to creating a nation's wealth and the big plus that my professors had said it was cracked up to be, then why weren't the more densely populated countries of the world the richest ones? How could Asia's seven big economies, supposedly bolstered by their mega-markets, which account for one quarter of the world's population, suddenly implode? I couldn't tear my eyes away from that map. I was determined to understand what was holding these countries back from prosperity.

Wars, famines, a lack of development capital, and ideological fingerpointing at the various sins of commission, omission, and oppression under the guises of — take your pick — imperialism, communism, capitalism: the age-old culprits, all the usual suspects, have provided tenure for countless diplomats, professors, librarians, and Pulitzer Prize–winning authors alike. Yet none had explained to my satisfaction why many countries and whole regions of the world have failed so utterly to develop beyond bare subsistence levels. Those that manage a leg up on the economic development ladder are just as likely to imitate Humpty Dumpty. Look at Asia.

There's no reason why large pools of the world's population should remain under-educated or illiterate in a knowledge economy. Creating a labour force with the most basic skills to support itself should be a goal for any country, especially with the abundance of funds available from official agencies and expansion-minded multinationals around the world today. "Why," I asked myself, "is it taking the world's developing nations *so* long to develop?"

Educating an entire population takes less than two decades, from the start of grade school to the attainment of a university degree. In the new knowledge economy, wouldn't it be pretty basic — or at least technologically and financially feasible — to aim to educate a couple of billion people long distance and mass produce that crucial knowledge base for the twenty-first century?

This process would shorten the usual length of time it takes to move people through the stages of economic development we recognized in the old economy.

Why would a nation not choose to invest in mass education to re-engineer economic development and give global growth a serious kickstart?

No economic law requires that generations toil at the margins of subsistence in the agrarian sector before expanding into some natural resource development, some basic industries, and a service sector. A nation does not require half a century to thrust itself upwards and onwards into mass manufacturing, advanced manufacturing, and high-knowledge services. Why not follow the lead of Ireland? Throw out the old economic-development rule books. Let's fast-forward into the knowledge economy. What is to prevent any nation from rewriting the rules of economic development? Why not focus on the global universality of a third-level education to meet the needs of a new, evolving economy?

Thinking all this through, I wandered back across the lobby for a cup of coffee. The UN's cafeteria would probably have had a hard time passing its World Health Organization's own standards.

By far the greatest roadblock I could deduce as I wandered around the United Nations building was one that every less developed and developing country must overcome — an insidious lack of *flexibility*. All the traditional reasons I could reel off why a country fails to adapt to changing conditions — to challenge its own ancient and deeply vested interests — amount to this: the process is always painful.

As a nine-year-old, I had stood in the same lobby, the same year that Nikita Khrushchev demanded the world's attention by taking off his shoe and pounding it on his desk. It was the same year that my father was transferred to New York to work at

39

Canada's mission to the UN. There I had had my first taste, however preliminary, of international economic development. Even at that tender age, I understood that, first and foremost, the rich rulers of poor countries preserved the old and vested interests that run deep within their institutions — cultural, social, religious, financial, and political.

The value of the gold braid that shimmered on many a general's uniform easily exceeded the industrial output of the country for which he sought aid.

As I stood in that same lobby nearly 35 years later, I suddenly understood Canada and its success in fresh terms. We Canadians have transformed ourselves from a social and economic backwater of the British Empire into the envy of the world in so many ways. We've accomplished this by building ourselves a solid foundation, too: we have demanded that our institutions and our society operate within a transparent, open, and flexible economy. We have dealt with lots of changes being thrown at us and have survived them. Our experiences have made us a stronger, more resilient, more open, and more innovative economy in every regard.

By the time I got back to my office in Toronto, I had worked out my research plan. I set to work.

North America stood in an enviable competitive position, I verified. First, I applied the major yardsticks on competitiveness from the prestigious international Institute for Management Development in Lausanne, Switzerland. These confirmed that Canada was moving with remarkable speed into the New Economy. By 1998, we had advanced from 20th place on IMD's world-competitiveness scoreboard to 10th place in only four years. Only Finland, which had pushed itself up from 19th place in 1994 to 5th this year, could claim a more impressive leap than Canada on to the top 10 list of the world's most competitive economies.

## World Competitiveness Scoreboard

| COUNTRY | 1998 RANKING |
|---|---|
| USA | 1 |
| Singapore | 2 |
| Hong Kong | 3 |
| Netherlands | 4 |
| Finland | 5 |
| Norway | 6 |
| Switzerland | 7 |
| Denmark | 8 |
| Luxembourg | 9 |
| Canada | 10 |

Source: Institute for Management
Development (www.IMD.ch)

I checked around other important research sources. Harvard University's Center for International Development, the OECD (Organization for Economic Cooperation and Development), the Council on Competitiveness, and the World Economic Forum at Davos in Switzerland confirmed Canada's high international standing and impressive competitive strengths.

Meanwhile our own research at Nuala Beck & Associates Inc. had identified four new, powerful, and essential sources of competitive advantage for the twenty-first century's knowledge economy. Each will dramatically affect and strengthen North America's role at the forefront of global growth.

# Advantage 1: Flexibility and Transparency

Is it mere coincidence that countries with the highest knowledge ratios have the lowest levels of corruption, and that those with the lowest knowledge ratios have the highest levels of corruption?

Hardly.

We were struck by the very clear relationship between knowledge and corruption levels around the world. The table on page

**41**

43 shows human development gone seriously off track and compares the corruption levels across 52 countries.

Transparency International is a leading and respected authority on international bribery and corruption, publishing these rankings annually. The links between higher knowledge and lower corruption, and lower knowledge and higher corruption are dramatic. (I recommend a visit to Transparency International's Berlin Web site at www.transparency.de. Their data are also useful clues to the indirect costs of doing business abroad. As the old saying goes, you can pay now ... or you can pay later — or "you can pay over the table ... or you can pay under the table" when it comes to the real cost of conducting business internationally.)

As high-knowledge countries thrive on openness, flexibility, and a willingness to challenge old and vested interests, so corrupt regimes are threatened by a sharply rising knowledge base. A higher knowledge economy will therefore find low levels of business corruption more to their advantage internationally.

As an aside, I urge Canada and other countries in the industrialized world to take a hard look at their foreign aid plans for the global knowledge economy of the twenty-first century. These nations would be wise to link their foreign aid directly to the receiving countries' efforts to promote and achieve basic education levels for their people. Hundreds of millions in foreign aid is currently being poured into regimes that cling to corruption and actually work to keep their citizens' knowledge base low in order to protect their own interests.

# Transparency International
# 1997 Corruption Perception Index
## (ranked from least corrupt to most corrupt)

| COUNTRY | 1997 | 1996 |
|---|---|---|
| 1. Denmark | 9.94 | 9.33 |
| 2. Finland | 9.48 | 9.05 |
| 3. Sweden | 9.35 | 9.08 |
| 4. New Zealand | 9.23 | 9.43 |
| 5. Canada | 9.10 | 8.96 |
| 6. Netherlands | 9.03 | 8.71 |
| 7. Norway | 8.92 | 8.87 |
| 8. Australia | 8.86 | 8.60 |
| 9. Singapore | 8.66 | 8.80 |
| 10. Luxembourg | 8.61 | — |
| 11. Switzerland | 8.61 | 8.76 |
| 12. Ireland | 8.28 | 8.45 |
| 13. Germany | 8.23 | 8.27 |
| 14. United Kingdom | 8.22 | 8.44 |
| 15. Israel | 7.97 | 7.71 |
| 16. United States | 7.61 | 7.66 |
| 17. Austria | 7.61 | 7.59 |
| 18. Hong Kong | 7.28 | 7.01 |
| 19. Portugal | 6.97 | 6.53 |
| 20. France | 6.66 | 6.96 |
| 21. Japan | 6.57 | 7.05 |
| 22. Costa Rica | 6.45 | — |
| 23. Chile | 6.05 | 6.80 |
| 24. Spain | 5.90 | 4.31 |
| 25. Greece | 5.35 | 5.01 |
| 26. Belgium | 5.25 | 6.84 |
| 27. Czech Republic | 5.20 | 5.37 |
| 28. Hungary | 5.18 | 4.86 |
| 29. Poland | 5.08 | 5.57 |
| 30. Italy | 5.03 | 3.42 |
| 31. Taiwan | 5.02 | 4.98 |
| 32. Malaysia | 5.01 | 5.32 |
| 33. South Africa | 4.95 | 5.68 |
| 34. South Korea | 4.29 | 5.02 |
| 35. Uruguay | 4.14 | — |
| 36. Brazil | 3.56 | 2.96 |
| 37. Romania | 3.44 | — |
| 38. Turkey | 3.21 | 3.54 |
| 39. Thailand | 3.06 | 3.33 |
| 40. Philippines | 3.05 | 2.69 |
| 41. China | 2.88 | 2.43 |
| 42. Argentina | 2.81 | 3.41 |
| 43. Vietnam | 2.79 | — |
| 44. Venezuela | 2.77 | 2.50 |
| 45. India | 2.75 | 2.63 |
| 46. Indonesia | 2.72 | 2.65 |
| 47. Mexico | 2.66 | 3.30 |
| 48. Pakistan | 2.53 | 1.00 |
| 49. Russia | 2.27 | 2.58 |
| 50. Columbia | 2.23 | 2.73 |
| 51. Bolivia | 2.05 | 3.40 |
| 52. Nigeria | 1.76 | 0.69 |

Source: Transparency International (www.transparency.de)

In the course of our firm's investigation, we detected another strong link as well: ethical countries who enjoy a high knowledge base also have the highest levels of human development in the world. The table on the preceding page ranks the 52 countries that Transparency International tracks in their annual survey of business corruption. Eighteen countries scored higher than 7.0 on the Corruption Perception Index (CPI), in which a score of 10 represents the least such corruption. These same countries ranked as the highest knowledge countries in the world.

| COUNTRY | Corruption Index 1997 (rank out of 52) | Knowledge Ratio 1996 (or last reporting period) (rank out of 40) | Human Development Index (rank out of 175) |
|---|---|---|---|
| Denmark | 1 | 36.7 (4) | 18 |
| Finland | 2 | 33.3 (10) | 8 |
| Sweden | 3 | 35.6 (7) | 10 |
| New Zealand | 4 | 36.2 (5) | 9 |
| Canada | 5 | 32.8 (11) | 1 |
| Netherlands | 6 | 44.1 (1) | 6 |
| Norway | 7 | 32.4 (12) | 3 |
| Australia | 8 | 24.9 (24) | 14 |
| Singapore | 9 | 37.3 (2) | 26 |
| Luxembourg | 10 | — | 27 |
| Switzerland | 11 | 19.8 (25) | 16 |
| Ireland | 12 | 31.2 (14) | 17 |
| Germany | 13 | 37.2 (3) | 19 |
| United Kingdom | 14 | 35.9 (6) | 15 |
| Israel | 15 | 30.9 (15) | 23 |
| United States | 16 | 31.9 (13) | 4 |
| Austria | 17 | 28.9 (17) | 12 |
| Hong Kong | 18 | 28.5 (18) | 22 |

Sources: Transparency International, ILO, Nuala Beck & Associates Inc.

Some on our list — Hungary, Spain, Belgium, and Poland — enjoy a moderately high knowledge base and are doing well in terms of economic growth and human development. However, we do question how well they will be able to sustain their economic progress when corruption runs rampant through much of business and government.

Too many Canadian companies and mutual fund investors learned the hard way that countries like Indonesia and South Korea are inherently unstable. (Think of Bre-X.) Countries on this list tend to either lurch from one economic and political crisis to the next or court such crises most of the time.

| COUNTRY | Corruption Index 1997 (rank out of 52) | Knowledge Ratio 1996 (or last reporting period) (rank out of 40) | Human Development Index (rank out of 175) |
|---|---|---|---|
| Portugal | 19 | 25.1 (23) | 31 |
| France | 20 | — | 2 |
| Japan | 21 | 16.1 (28) | 7 |
| Costa Rica | 22 | — | 33 |
| Chile | 23 | 12.0 (32) | 30 |
| Spain | 24 | 27.5 (19) | 11 |
| Greece | 25 | 27.0 (20) | 20 |
| Belgium | 26 | 26.3 (22) | 13 |
| Czech Republic | 27 | 34.0 (9) | 39 |
| Hungary | 28 | 29.4 (16) | 48 |
| Poland | 29 | 26.7 (21) | 58 |
| Italy | 30 | 10.6 (33) | 21 |
| Taiwan | 31 | — | — |
| Malaysia | 32 | 13.5 (31) | 60 |
| South Africa | 33 | — | 90 |
| South Korea | 34 | 17.0 (27) | 32 |
| Uruguay | 35 | — | 37 |

Sources: Transparency International, ILO, Nuala Beck & Associates Inc.

Perhaps, like me, you are surprised to see France and Italy keeping such questionable company. In fact, France is deteriorating even further than this. As its competitive position declines, it is coming under mounting pressure to restructure its economy — move out of the industries of the old economy and into the new. France's competitive position plummeted on IMD's 1998 scorecard, from 13th place in 1994 to 21st position. Italy, too, slid from 28th place to 30th, suggesting that both countries' economic and financial situations could unravel further with lightning speed.

While both France and Italy enjoy the helpful cushion of Europe's large internal market to keep their economies and financial systems reasonably stable, an advantage that Japan lacked, I doubt either country will adapt smoothly to the high-knowledge world. Change is difficult enough under any circumstances. A country finds it harder and harder to adapt when it closes its eyes to corruption or allows it to cloud the national vision and agenda.

I have said that the most corrupt countries in the world display the lowest knowledge ratios on earth. For all their rhetoric, promises, and pleas for aid and understanding, the entrenched status quo of these nations is not prepared to accept any large improvements in their countries' knowledge base.

| COUNTRY | Corruption Index 1997 (rank out of 52) | Knowledge Ratio 1996 (or last reporting period) (rank out of 40) | Human Development Index (rank out of 175) |
|---|---|---|---|
| Brazil | 36 | 7.5 (36) | 68 |
| Romania | 37 | — | 79 |
| Turkey | 38 | 7.8 (34) | 74 |
| Thailand | 39 | — | 59 |
| Philippines | 40 | 7.6 (35) | 98 |
| China | 41 | — | 108 |
| Argentina | 42 | — | 36 |
| Vietnam | 43 | — | 121 |
| Venezuela | 44 | 15.7 (29) | 47 |
| India | 45 | — | 138 |
| Indonesia | 46 | — | 99 |
| Mexico | 47 | 15.5 (30) | 50 |
| Pakistan | 48 | 6.0 (38) | 139 |
| Russia | 49 | — | 67 |
| Columbia | 50 | — | 51 |
| Bolivia | 51 | — | 113 |
| Nigeria | 52 | — | 141 |

Sources: Transparency International, ILO, Nuala Beck & Associates Inc.

# Advantage 2: The Electronic Immigrant

Every great era of growth has been fuelled by the investment of human capital in some form. In less civilized times, slavery was common. This very literal employment of human capital meant nations could build their economies rapidly, through a simple exchange of the bare necessities of life in return for back-breaking labour.

Over the centuries, a phenomenal social, legal, and economic transition gradually transformed slavery into indenture, which in turn gave way to a system of voluntary apprenticeship and then the current system of free labour markets. Any country wishing to speed up the process of increasing its population and labour force looked more and more to immigration as one means to accomplish this.

Countries like Canada attracted large numbers of immigrants by offering them cheap or even free land. For more than half of this century, Canada offered to pay the passage of immigrants, many of whom could not afford the fares themselves.

To meet the many and varied demands of growth, many countries, such as Canada, adopted a minimum wage through legislation. This guaranteed all members of society the necessities for survival — food, clothing, shelter, and little more. Particularly since the early 1960s, many societies have seen large numbers of "guest workers" (in Germany) and illegal immigrants (in the United States) supplement the domestic workforce. In the case of the United States, Mexican migrant workers work in agriculture, meat processing, and textiles, low-wage industries that no longer attract American workers. The latter have found better opportunities on the production lines of the country's industrial heartland.

Countries have come to recognize that they can attract the human capital they need to sustain their growth without shouldering all of the social costs that their own citizens have come to

47

expect. The bonus? Low-wage, low-knowledge, and fundamentally non-competitive industries can remain in business by paying less than a minimum wage to its workforce. During the 1960s and 1970s, Germany and Switzerland relied heavily on "guest workers" from Yugoslavia, Turkey, and southern Italy in low-skilled jobs. But these guest workers inevitably required food and shelter and a broad range of social services. In the end, they cost governments much more than expected.

As our economy changes, in yet another twist of history, the electronic immigrant is now set to burst onto this scene. The new wave of these electronic immigrants will be to the next century what guest workers were to Europe at the end of this one, and what migrant workers were and are today to the United States.

But there is a **key** difference.

Highly educated knowledge workers are "networked." They enjoy a world of choices unavailable to their immigrant predecessors. This technology, which allows people to connect and communicate with one another from different locations, is profoundly changing the nature of immigration. It is also changing the way business is conducted everywhere. Companies woo these workers aggressively and must treat them well as coveted corporate assets.

Highly educated electronic immigrants will fill job vacancies and boost production while drawing on costly education, health, and social services at home. The wealth-creating impact of these electronic immigrants on their host countries promises to exceed that of guest workers. No social, medical, or education costs are attached to these immigrants. They show up for work online and use all the social, medical, and educational services they need in their home countries. Electronic immigrants will shift the balance of global power by enriching host countries like Canada and the United States. They represent pure profit to the companies and nations that employ them.

Countries such as New Zealand, Singapore, and most of Nordic Europe (Denmark, Iceland, Finland, and Norway) all score well in our country knowledge ratio rankings, and will become important sources of this new kind of high-end immigration in the twenty-first century.

Even countries with a low knowledge base are providing electronic immigrants to North America. At Hyderabad in India, a new high-tech city centred around the Indian Institute for Information Technology, companies such as Microsoft and Metamor Worldwide are setting a trend in establishing company-sponsored universities. In return for first choice in recruiting these graduates, the companies furnish the instructors and they in turn equip their students with specific knowledge so that they hit the ground running in their employment on graduation.

Such graduates learn to design computer systems and pound out computer code at astounding rates, applying the latest technology. Some of Canada's second-tier universities and community colleges don't even offer such technology — and may never be able to afford it.

International comparisons of students and their achievements are breaking down competition around the world, from grade school on up. These comparisons are published frequently, prompting both parents and policy-makers to ask why some of their countries' students can read while others cannot, regardless of class size or funding budget per pupil. The knowledge economy demands that transparent standards be applied worldwide. Education cannot be allowed as an exception.

Canada still faces a long road before it in rethinking the way it educates its people. The University of Western Ontario, for example, is moving miles ahead of many with its faculty of engineering. The university now offers an innovative combined-degree program in medicine and engineering. This equips young engineers with a degree in medicine and prepares them for the medical-technology industry of the next century, one of the four high-knowledge industries that are driving growth in our economy. (The other three engines are computers and semiconductors; communications and telecommunications, and instrumentation.)

However high in quality certain degree or diploma programs may be, the real issue of educating Canadians for the New Economy has barely begun to be addressed. It's only a matter of time until Canada's *real* revolution in education really gets under way.

Canadians of all ages upgrade their skills at community colleges through distance-education and high school courses of every description. Picture distance-education, now in its infancy, shifting into high gear. As educational institutions learn to apply existing technologies more effectively, improved education, the higher revenues luring institutions to adapt to these developments, and the billions of dollars in administrative and capital cost savings will profoundly affect our economy. The savings alone could propel Canada to offer free networked university and community college programs to its residents in the early years of the next century.

## Advantage 3: The English Language

New and powerful competitive advantages are emerging. Anyone who can surf the Internet enjoys a head start over those who have not hooked up to it yet. Those with a command of English enjoy a particularly powerful advantage as the English language dominates this age of information and networking.

In the forthcoming century, the Internet will become the platform for electronic commerce even as it is now the platform for the global exchange of information. And North America is perfectly positioned to control this brave new business world.

McKinsey, the highly respected U.S. consulting firm, has estimated that the United States could increase its gross domestic product by a full third by the year 2005 as businesses and organizations employ the technologies they already have in place. The power of intranets (which link companies internally), extranets (which link their external suppliers to them), and the Internet (which provides customer access) will change life as we know it. In a recent report entitled *The Emerging Digital Economy*, the U.S. Department of Commerce cites the following examples to describe this online explosion:

- Fewer than 40 million people around the world were connected to the Internet during 1996. By the end of 1997, that number had mushroomed to more than 100 million people.
- As of December 1996, about 627,000 Internet domain names had been registered. By the end of 1997, that number had skyrocketed to more than double, 1.5 million.
- Traffic on the Internet has been doubling every 100 days.
- Cisco Systems, the giant U.S. systems integrator, ended 1996 having booked slightly more than $100 million in sales on the Internet. By the end of 1997, those sales were running at $3.2 billion annually.
- In 1996, Amazon.com, the first Internet bookstore, recorded sales of less than $16 million. In 1997, it sold $148 million worth of books to Internet customers. Accordingly, one of the nation's largest book retailers, Barnes and Noble, launched its own online bookstore in 1997 to compete with Amazon for this rapidly growing market.
- In January 1997, Dell Computers was selling less than $1 million worth of computers each day on the Internet. During the December holiday period of the same year, the company reported daily sales of $6 million several times.
- A Web-based automotive marketplace, Auto-by-Tel, processed 345,000 purchase requests through its site in 1996, or $1.8

billion in auto sales. As of the end of November 1997, the site was generating $500 million a month ($6 billion annualized) and processing more than 100,000 purchase requests each month.

• Late into the game, Microsoft has sparked controversy with their big Internet push as the U.S. government recognizes the power of any company that effectively controls Internet access.

Canadians already enjoy the lowest Internet connect charges in the world: a recent flyer in the mail offered access at $2.99 per month, and at last glance Bell's Sympatico charged about $10 per month for Internet access. Balanced against this advantage, Canada's higher than forty-cents-an-hour wage rates just don't mean what they once did.

# Advantage 4: Quality of Life

Any employee considering relocation for the sake of employment takes quality of life into account for his or her family. Now countries are recognizing superior quality of life as a greater, even key, strategic advantage to their ability to attract increasingly mobile knowledge workers. And this category of workers is expanding exponentially. Current statistics demonstrate a shortage of as many as 2,000 knowledge workers in selected high-technology industries in Canada alone. Staffing companies in America are turning their attention abroad for software professionals as their own country encounters critical shortages.

As Canada's economy grows, it will absorb our own pool of knowledge workers, and companies will seek more and more of these workers wherever they can find them. For example, a recent

*Globe and Mail* article documented a Halifax-based software company which offered a reward of $1,000 to anyone who recruited a successful candidate to fill a knowledge worker position.

The list of knowledge ratio rankings on page 56 also makes informative reading for immigration officials and human resource managers alike. The table strongly suggests that executive search companies comb through those countries with higher knowledge bases than our own, and where the standard of living and well-being is lower. The Human Development Index, which measures this, lists countries such as Denmark as potentially good pools of this kind of worker. The opportunities Canada holds out for these people and their children make Canada a very attractive destination for the twenty-first century.

As knowledge workers within Canada become increasingly in short supply many of our high-knowledge companies may find boat- and plane-loads of people arriving from Denmark, Singapore, and Finland most welcome. To compete effectively, companies will need to build up their staff quickly and may not be able to use electronic immigration channels because not every job in the knowledge economy can be carried out from a distance. In this context, a country's success may come to be defined in terms of its retention of its own asset base of these workers, and its strength in competing with other countries for them.

In the 1950s and 1960s, countries pursued foreign direct investment vigorously. Many welcomed multinationals with open arms. By the 1970s and early 1980s, this emphasis had shifted to a country's ability to attract capital and financial investment. Interest rates became an important means to attract this influx of money. Throughout the 1980s, a country's potential for growth increasingly depended on its success in securing access to foreign markets for its goods and services. Hence the negotiation and signing of various international trade agreements at the time.

Since the 1980s and in the last years of this decade, the definition of economic growth has been transformed yet again. Observers now look at a country's capacity to educate a workforce of knowledge workers, keep them happy at home, and lure the knowledge workers it needs from other countries, either in person or as electronic immigrants.

Communities in North America have already had some taste of what it takes to persuade these high-knowledge companies to establish themselves here and keep them. For many corporations, the means of succeeding in the New Economy will equal managing this knowledge effectively.

The table on the next page condenses the United Nations' rankings of its Human Resource Development Index for 175 countries.

## United Nations 1997 Human Resource Development Index

| UNITED NATIONS RANK | COUNTRY |
|:---:|:---|
| 1 | **Canada** |
| 2 | France |
| 3 | Norway |
| 4 | **United States** |
| 5 | Iceland |
| 6 | Netherlands |
| 7 | Japan |
| 8 | Finland |
| 9 | New Zealand |
| 10 | Sweden |
| 15 | United Kingdom |
| 17 | Ireland |
| 19 | Germany |
| 22 | Hong Kong |
| 26 | Singapore |
| 32 | Korea |
| 50 | Mexico |
| 59 | Thailand |
| 60 | Malaysia |
| 98 | Philippines |
| 99 | Indonesia |
| 138 | India |

Source: www.undp.org

The data are as relevant as they are interesting. Twenty-first–century success will depend in part on how desirable certain countries or locations are to knowledge workers who are considering whether or not to live there either full- or part-time. Just as our resource companies once paid hefty wage premiums to workers to attract them to move to remote northern areas, so high-knowledge companies could realize significant savings in attracting these workers to Canada.

With knowledge workers accounting for 32.8 percent of its labour force in 1996, Canada runs the risk of a considerable brain drain to the United States. Similarly, other countries will find themselves vulnerable to aggressive recruiting by Canadian companies. The table on the next page indicates countries with a

55

high proportion of knowledge workers residing in countries whose scores are lower than Canada's on the Human Resource Development Index — offering their residents less attractive living conditions. These countries are and will be particularly susceptible to employee poaching. To Canada they represent a potentially good source of knowledge workers.

## Recruitment Pool of Knowledge Workers

| UNITED NATIONS RANK | KNOWLEDGE RANK (%) | COUNTRY |
|---|---|---|
| 1 | 32.8 | Canada |
| 5 | 35.0 | Iceland |
| 8 | 33.3 | Finland |
| 9 | 36.2 | New Zealand |
| 10 | 35.6 | Sweden |
| 26 | 37.3 | Singapore |

Sources:  United Nations Human Development Index and
Nuala Beck & Associates Inc.

The information age holds out the promise of a truly global, borderless labour market. Younger, less experienced workers, of course, would likely encounter some restrictions on their mobility until they achieved sufficient experience to wield some negotiating power in such a market. As a result of this, we could see a two-tier labour pool emerging; companies would enjoy ready access to the seasoned knowledge workers they need while simultaneously grappling with a pronounced shortage of younger workers coming along behind them. This interpretation would correspond with North America's current demographic trends, and the slower growth of our labour force.

In any event, the globalization we think we have come to know is about to end. These shifts in world labour markets and other aspects of the New Economy signal intense fragmentation and change. Those companies and investors who understand their underlying significance and the possibilities ahead will have a head start over those that don't.

# 3

# CHASING THE
# GLOBAL RAINBOW

In the summer of 1997 I opened the file our research team had compiled and stared at my computer screen, puzzled by the numbers I was scrolling through.

The telephone jarred me away from the numbers. It was Joseph Connolly, our head of research, calling to tell me he had just compiled more tables with data that fell into the "must-see" category. He passed me the tables electronically; I opened the first one to discover that, incredibly, his figures showed that 38 North American industries — 15 of them in Canada — were growing larger and faster than the fastest-growing economies on Earth.

Most important to me, though, was the return-to-risk analysis Joseph had sent. This analysis measures the stability and predictability of that growth. After months of sifting through thousands of pages of international and industry data, my team and I knew we were watching North America's knowledge economy winning the global race hands down. Canada and the United States were poised to dominate the first half of the twenty-first century.

I thought through the vast implications of our findings. How deeply globalization has become entrenched in our minds as an entire creed of economic faith. Thousands of companies were committing precious working capital and scarce management resources to regions of the world that they believed would offer their shareholders the highest rates of growth and returns.

Through our compilations we had identified an imminent sea change. From mutual funds and marketing to joint ventures and partnerships, a decisive shift would soon begin — *away* from globalization as a major force driving corporate strategy. Instead, companies across a vast range of North American industries would soon begin to concentrate their marketing, investment, and management energies back into home markets as never before.

Why? Because investment return-to-risk profiles into the twenty-first century would demand nothing less.

And that changes everything.

Take a look at the numbers. They will likely change the way you see your world as much as they have ours. You'll learn to recognize the broader significance of North America's New Economy to the global economy, to corporate strategy, and to Canada's future.

# Blind Faith

Imagine you are in a spacecraft making its final re-entry into the Earth's atmosphere. You are watching the heavens around you, filled with stars, as the shapes of great oceans and continents loom ever larger ahead. In the early 1960s, America was the land of promise and possibility. It was the powerful nation that could dare to land a man on the moon. As poor cousins, Canadians looked on with awe and envy.

If asked today, many North Americans would probably identify China and India as "emerging economies," the top contenders for economic success in the twenty-first century. Individual Canadians constantly face the decision about where to invest our RRSPs and how best to save for our retirement years. Companies large and small have to decide where to allocate capital and resources across a vast marketplace and try to determine the best possible export markets for their products.

However, when it comes to economic growth, Canada and the United States already lead the G-7. But despite our economic triumphs as a nation, as we prepare ourselves for a new millenium, that's not how most people see things at all.

You could call the "Decline of the American Empire" the longest-running melodrama in history. Education, family values, social policy, public safety: each and all are seen as the root cause(s), or the result, of economic and financial decline. This vague impression is accepted as proof that the best is behind us now. Companies across North America have convinced themselves that they will never enjoy sustained and vigorous growth in home markets as they once did. Worse, companies and investors believe they have no choice but to trek through the jungles of Malaysia or join some junta-of-the-month club in countries whose names we would have been hard-pressed to spell correctly just 20 years ago.

The conventional wisdom of most boardroom tables remains bred in our bones, the idea that North America's economic and financial prowess have faded. Every aspect of corporate life has been restructured — barring corporate Canada's belief system. In the last two decades, companies have restructured, reengineered, refinanced, and reorganized themselves, some of them many times over. From customer service to production, distribution to purchasing, everything within the modern corporation has been challenged and ultimately changed. Only the inner sanctum of faith in globalization remains untouched.

We see our highly industrialized economies tottering along in old age, the mature phase of our growth cycle. Little wonder the vigorous growth of our 1990s economy has been viewed with such deep suspicion! Most North Americans have tacitly accepted that the future belongs to the emerging markets of the world, especially those centred around Asia Pacific, not to us. Never mind those countries' "growing pains," as one wag in the Wall Street Journal described the entire region's current financial collapse.

From Roman times right through to the British Empire, we have been taught that history is littered with remnants and ideas of great economic powers, the rise of each inevitably matched by its eventual fall. As strongly as any article of religious faith, we cling to the notion that this century's American empire will be unseated and displaced. The only questions are "When" and "By whom"?

Since the late 1960s when the United States reached the peak of its influence in Henry Ford's automobile age, it has been fashionable to nod knowingly at the prospect that the best in North America is behind us. Recent history shores up this expectation:

- OPEC's Arab sheiks regularly graced the pages of *Time* and *Newsweek* in the early 1970s. It was widely assumed that the oil kingdoms would control international financial markets through the mammoth recycling of their petro-dollars. When that prediction didn't pan out, the money experts moved on to the next headlines, which turned up surprisingly closer to home.
- In the late 1970s, South America became the investment miracle du jour, led by Brazil. International analysts promoting vast econometric models proselytized fervently that South America would power a growth miracle that would change the world. If these soothsayers had left off their predictions at that point, enjoyed a couple of margaritas, and headed home from Carnival tanned and spent — and with their life savings

and ours safely stowed in the vault — all would have ended well. Instead, these wizards fanned the inflation fires of South America to 2,000 percent and higher, fuelled by the billions of dollars in international capital squandered.

- By the mid-eighties, large armies of experts were dispatched to the Pacific Rim. This time, Japan looked like the economic miracle everyone had been waiting for. Flexing breathtaking muscles, the tiny nation fed into a media and investment frenzy. Japan could do no wrong. Canadians compared themselves to this Asian giant as lazy, greedy, less intelligent — altogether inferior. Japan Inc. was destined to inherit the earth.
- The late 1980s saw the dawning of a great new age for Europe. Germany's reunification triggered this, closely followed by the opening up of the East Bloc and the prospect of a monetary union being forged among European Community members. Never mind euro-fuddle and the Moscow Mafia.
- In the 1990s the same wizards looked to the emerging economies of Asia Pacific. The entire region now operates as little more than an IMF protectorate.

All these fads only go to show that what our parents always reminded us is true: "The grass is always greener on the other side."

## The Emerging Global Recession

Astute observers — and readers — will notice that every time we reach the end of a global rainbow, the world's economies plunge into recession. Many economists persist in dismissing the economic collapse of Asia as a short-term tempest in a teapot.

Meanwhile, Canada's resource sector is folding like a house of cards. British Columbia was the first to slide into recession as a virulent strain of the Asian flu struck. Mining, forestry, tourism,

**61**

and construction in the province are in trouble. The leaky condo fiasco and its devastating impact on consumer confidence in B.C. could not have come at a worse time, which only goes to show that in economics it doesn't rain, but it pours.

Alberta's oil patch has felt the domino effect of collapsing commodity prices already. Sinking international oil prices have been mitigated by firm North American pricing for natural gas. The farsighted company strategists shifted to natural gas years ago. At the same time, Saskatchewan's potash industry, which exports almost one-third of its production to the Pacific Rim, will likely be caught in the Asian crisis fallout, too.

Wide-eyed optimists believe the Pacific Rim will spring back soon. These people are heading for serious disappointment. For Canada, the impact is rippling through our economy now. With three of its 10 provinces threatened by prolonged recession, Canada is slowly discovering that its resource industries and suppliers will remain troubled until they can restructure their export markets and move aggressively into the U.S. market.

Be grateful that the United States has been busily building itself a powerhouse of an economy. It's happened right under our noses.

# The New Reality

Forget Europe. Forget Japan. Forget China and the Asian Tigers. Why? Because North America is where the action is, and it is positioned to dominate for the first half of the next century.

Here are a few of the new realities that pave the way to this continent's global dominance:

• The U.S. semiconductor industry is larger than the entire economy of Singapore. It's also growing three times faster.

- The instrumentation industry — process-control equipment, robotics, laboratory instruments, and the like — is larger than the economies of Singapore and the Philippines combined.
- Microsoft's market capitalization of more than US$200 billion exceeds the entire gross domestic product of Hong Kong.
- General Electric has a market capitalization of almost US$260 billion, which, when combined with Microsoft's market capitalization of over US$250 billion, exceeds the gross domestic product of Argentina and Colombia.
- The medical technology and supply industry in the United States is expected to double in the next five years. This industry has surpassed the high-knowledge economy of Finland in size.
- BCE's market capitalization of more than US$25 billion exceeds Luxembourg's GDP.
- With 55.0 telephone lines per 100 inhabitants, Canada has more access to information than India, Indonesia, Philippines, Thailand, Malaysia, and China put together.
- In Canada, 15 industries, and another 23 in the United States, are already generating higher return-to-risk than what *The Economist* and *Business Week* only recently regarded as the fastest growing economies on Earth.
- America's knowledge base, with 31.9 knowledge workers per 100 employees, is more than double that of Mexico, which is 15.5.
- Despite the United States' success, Canada has a higher knowledge base. With 32.8 knowledge workers per 100 employees, Canada has nearly double the proportion of knowledge workers that Japan does, at 16.1, and more than three times as many proportionately as the Philippines, at 7.6.

The table below demonstrates the sheer might of North America's high-knowledge industries against the world's emerging economies.

Can we Canadians avoid a long and deep recession? I cannot overemphasize my answer: These industries are the only hope we have.

## North America's High-Knowledge Engines versus Emerging Economies

| 1996 | US$ BILLIONS |
|---|---|
| 1. China | 700.6 |
| 2. Korea | 478.5 |
| 3. Taiwan | 272.5 |
| 4. U.S. Information Technology | 251.0 |
| 5. U.S. Instrumentation Industry | 150.6 |
| 6. U.S. Semiconductor Industry | 125.3 |
| 7. U.S. Healthcare Products | 123.4 |
| 8. U.S. Computer Industry | 104.3 |
| 9. Singapore | 85.3 |
| 10. U.S. Comm. & Tel. Industry | 72.3 |
| 11. Malaysia | 72.3 |
| 12. Philippines | 23.9 |
| 13. Cdn. Telecommunications | 14.5 |
| 14. Cdn. Electronic Equipment | 3.9 |
| 15. Cdn. Computer Industry | 3.4 |

Source: International Monetary Fund, U.S. Dept. of Commerce, and Statistics Canada

# The Growth Hunters

Quick — what do the following companies have in common? Hewlett Packard — Bell Canada — General Motors — Texas Instruments — Warner Music Group — Caterpillar Inc. — General Electric — Proctor and Gamble — Unisys Corp. — Whirlpool Corp. — Virgin Retail.

Okay. All of them recently backed away from joint ventures in regions of the world that were supposed to be high-growth areas. As can be imagined, many of them lost hundreds of millions of dollars in the process.

Over the course of the 1990s, American and Canadian companies and individual investors have dumped billions of dollars into Asia. They did so with every reasonable expectation of earning a handsome return for their shareholders, and building themselves a solid base of earnings into the next millennium.

Alas, in their rush for global growth, they forgot or did not know that all earnings are not created equal. In the last 50 years, companies have sifted carefully through the world's economies in the hopes of turning up promising emerging markets most likely to grow and profit. Companies of all sizes have allocated scarce resources to countries hinting at large returns. But, like GM, Bell Canada, and Virgin Retail, they couldn't have made a worse bet.

## The China Syndrome

The world's auto makers converged on China in the early 1990s, lured by the prospect of getting in on the ground floor of a large and rapidly expanding market. The rich possibility of producing three million cars annually over the next decade made the industry drool. Average Chinese workers were seeing their incomes double every seven years. "China's potential is just tremendous," auto analysts gushed, happily spouting statistics on China's real growth rate, which averaged 14.6 percent in the last five years alone. The huge nation represented a $700-billion economy, as analysts measured it in U.S. dollars.

But hang on a second. Hold everything!

Companies that have chased the global rainbow from Brazil to Bahrain and back ought to look before they leap yet again. To date they have lost billions of hard-earned profit margins that investors like you and me have committed to their corporate coffers. In the vast engines of the New Economy driving U.S. economic growth has arisen a larger, safer, and more lucrative market — of knowledge workers.

In the 10 years between 1987 and 1997, the mighty U.S. economy created 14,686,000 new high-knowledge jobs net of those jobs that may have fallen by the wayside. From an automaker's perspective, you would think that should have piqued interest: highly paid knowledge workers accustomed to the best and fastest technology drool over the techno-gizmos that are *not* packed into their latest-model vehicles. Compared with an existing car market of fewer than 400,000 cars in China that *might* grow to 3 million in another 10 years, America's market of more than 14 million *new* knowledge workers stands out as a segment worth some attention. Surely those numbers suggest that the industry incorporate some innovation into its products and accordingly its marketing and sales.

Paul, a typical modern knowledge worker and a family friend, told me how he interpreted North American car manufacturers and their products: "I work in a high-tech business park next to companies like SHL, Bell Mobility, Hewlett-Packard, BaaN, Silicon Graphics. All the cutting-edge technology is inside the buildings we work in, while all the old technology is left sitting outside in the parking lot.

"Don't the automakers realize just how frustrating it is to be stuck behind the wheel of one of their cars, after spending hours at work with instant access to information, on my terms, when I need it? Or do they just not care about meeting customer needs except in developing countries where the customers have very low expectations to begin with?

"Except for my commuting time to and from work, I spend most of my waking hours connected to the most powerful information systems and search engines on Earth. But once I get into my 4X4, it's pathetic, really. You need a sense of humour when you turn on the car radio to hear the latest traffic report or, worse yet, reach for the old road map to find your way after missing a turn.

"It doesn't take a rocket scientist to master technology. Trouble is, most of the line people I meet in business want as little to do with the IT crowd as possible. They don't realize that we are their market.

"I'm not an automotive engineer, but as a software developer I reckon that all they would really have to do is take out the ancient radio and air-conditioning dials and replace them with a touch screen monitor that houses the air-conditioning controls, the car's system diagnostics, as well as the online system that will link me up to a PCS phone, a GPS (global positioning service), and a high-speed cell modem. With that on board I would have access to the local CAA server and a host of information services I could really use, like www.vicinity.com and www.whowhere.com, my favourite online services for street-level mapping and directions. A whole new market could be created for radio stations by enabling me to listen to any station in the world, instead of being limited to the local ones. Looking for the cheapest gas or closest Starbucks, McDonald's, or ATM would be a breeze and would make excellent use of existing Web sites, like www.yahoo.ca or www.canoe.ca.

"Functional services that didn't make my time driving my vehicle any less enjoyable would be a blessing. I'd be happy to spend a bit more on a 'smart car' if it could be as intelligent as my workplace has already become."

Four industry engines drive the knowledge economy: computers and semiconductors; instrumentation; health and medical technology; and communications and telecommunications. It's high time companies reassessed the more lucrative returns gaining momentum right in their own backyards.

# The First Engine

The U.S. computer and semiconductor industry ships $230-billion worth of its technology all over the world. This engine alone in the United States surpasses the entire economy of Indonesia in size, which economists have long touted as a growth miracle.

# The Second Engine

The instrumentation industry in the United States is a $150-billion business. Imagine a single U.S. industry almost as large as the gross national product of Norway. This industry's payroll of more than $33 billion feeds a high-knowledge labour market in which almost 46 percent of its employees are highly paid knowledge workers.

# The Third and Fourth Engines

The American medical equipment and products industry generates US$123 billion — making it larger than the entire economy of Greece. Add on the Comm. & Tel. (communications and telecommunications) equipment industry's US$72 billion worth of shipments and you begin to get some feel for these lucrative industries.

These four high-knowledge engines are moving and shaking the whole business scene — computers and semiconductors; health and medical technology; communications and telecommunications; and instrumentation. The four alone account for US$575 billion in revenues — and by any conventional economist's abacus, that's larger than Korea's $400-billion economy.

Businesses extol the virtues of the educated consumer all the time, those with high and rising incomes coupled with strong shopping instincts. Banks trip all over themselves to serve this profitable market. Yet, when it comes to business basics and being able to distinguish between what's growing and what's not, or the specific quality and characteristics of that growth, it's hard to imagine any of them having taken a basic marketing course. If they had, surely they could recognize that China's eye-popping growth of 14.6 percent in the last five years and 9.6 percent in the last 10 years has been ground to pieces by the enormous volatility of that same growth. Growth that is intrinsically volatile, as China's has been over the last one year, three, five, and 10 years can erase a lot of zeroes on a company's bottom line. It is common sense to take the trouble to calculate the return-to-risk of investing in industries, countries, and particular regions of the world. If companies had bothered to do that with any degree of systematic analysis, their research would confirm what I'm about to show you.

## 5-Year Growth

| (IN US $) | GROWTH (%) |
|---|---|
| 1. Singapore | 16.7 |
| 2. China | 14.6 |
| 3. Malaysia | 13.8 |
| 4. U.S. Comm. and Tel. | 13.7 |
| 5. U.S. Semiconductor Industry | 13.2 |
| 6. Philippines | 12.1 |
| 7. Cdn. Computer Industry | 11.9 |
| 8. U.S. Computer Industry | 11.4 |
| 9. Korea | 9.8 |
| 10. U.S. Information Technology | 9.3 |
| 11. Cdn. Electronic Equipment | 8.3 |
| 12. Taiwan | 7.8 |
| 13. Cdn. Telecommunications | 7.6 |
| 14. U.S. Medical Equipment and Products | 5.6 |
| 15. U.S. Instrumentation Industry | 2.5 |

**What the Numbers Reveal**

Growth in U.S. Four-Engine Industries is strengthening structurally: from an average rate of 7.3 percent over 10 years to 9.3 percent over 5 years.

## 10-Year Growth

| (IN US $) | GROWTH (%) |
|---|---|
| 1. Singapore | 16.6 |
| 2. Korea | 15.2 |
| 3. Taiwan | 13.4 |
| 4. Cdn. Computer Industry | 12.9 |
| 5. U.S. Semiconductor Industry | 11.6 |
| 6. Philippines | 11.3 |
| 7. China | 9.6 |
| 8. Cdn. Telecommunications | 8.2 |
| 9. U.S. Medical Equipment and Products | 8.2 |
| 10. Malaysia | 8.2 |
| 11. U.S. Comm. and Tel. | 7.9 |
| 12. Cdn. Electronic Equipment | 6.4 |
| 13. U.S. Computer Industry | 6.1 |
| 14. U.S. Information Technology | 6.1 |
| 15. U.S. Instrumentation Industry | 4.1 |

Sources: International Monetary Fund, U.S. Department of Commerce, Statistics Canada, and Nuala Beck & Associates Inc.

# 5-Year Volatility
## (Ranked by standard deviation
## from least volatile to most volatile)

| (IN US $) | VOLATILITY |
|---|---|
| 1. U.S. Instrumentation Industry | 0.2 |
| 2. U.S. Medical Equipment and Products | 0.3 |
| 3. U.S. Information Technology | 0.4 |
| 4. U.S. Computer Industry | 0.5 |
| 5. U.S. Comm. and Tel. | 0.5 |
| 6. U.S. Semiconductor Industry | 0.6 |
| 7. Cdn. Telecommunications | 0.9 |
| 8. Korea | 1.9 |
| 9. Cdn. Electronic Equipment | 3.9 |
| 10. Malaysia | 3.9 |
| 11. Taiwan | 4.6 |
| 12. Cdn. Computer Industry | 6.2 |
| 13. Singapore | 6.4 |
| 14. Philippines | 11.5 |
| 15. China | 15.7 |

# 10-Year Volatility
## (Ranked by standard deviation
## from least volatile to most volatile)

| (IN US $) | VOLATILITY |
|---|---|
| 1. U.S. Instrumentation Industry | 0.2 |
| 2. U.S. Medical Equipment and Products | 0.3 |
| 3. U.S. Information Technology | 0.5 |
| 4. U.S. Semiconductor Industry | 0.6 |
| 5. U.S. Comm. and Tel. | 0.7 |
| 6. U.S. Computer Industry | 0.8 |
| 7. Cdn. Telecommunications | 1.0 |
| 8. Korea | 3.0 |
| 9. Cdn. Electronic Equipment | 3.4 |
| 10. Cdn. Computer Industry | 5.8 |
| 11. Malaysia | 9.2 |
| 12. Singapore | 9.3 |
| 13. Philippines | 11.1 |
| 14. Taiwan | 11.6 |
| 15. China | 13.6 |

**What the Numbers Reveal**

Volatility in U.S. Four-Engine Industries has historically been low: from an average standard deviation of 0.5 on a 10-year basis, to 0.4 on a five-year basis.

Sources: International Monetary Fund, U.S. Department of Commerce, Statistics Canada, and Nuala Beck & Associates Inc.

71

# 5-Year Return-to-Risk
## (Coefficient of variation from highest return
## and lowest risk to lowest return and highest risk)

| (IN US $) | RETURN-TO-RISK RATIO |
|---|---|
| 1.  U.S. Comm. and Tel. Industry | 25.5 |
| 2.  U.S. Information Technology | 24.5 |
| 3.  U.S. Semiconductor Industry | 22.8 |
| 4.  U.S. Computer Industry | 21.8 |
| 5.  U.S. Medical Equipment and Products | 21.8 |
| 6.  U.S. Instrumentation Industry | 14.5 |
| 7.  Cdn. Telecommunications | 8.5 |
| 8.  Korea | 5.2 |
| 9.  Malaysia | 3.5 |
| 10.  Singapore | 2.6 |
| 11.  Cdn. Electronic Equipment | 2.1 |
| 12.  Cdn. Computer Industry | 1.9 |
| 13.  Taiwan | 1.7 |
| 14.  Philippines | 1.0 |
| 15.  China | 0.9 |

**What the
Numbers
Reveal**

Return-to-Risk
in U.S. Four-
Engine
Industries is
increasing
structurally: from
a coefficient of
variation of 16.4
on a 10-year
basis, to 21.8 on a
five-year basis.

# 10-Year Return-to-Risk
## (Coefficient of variation from highest return
## and lowest risk to lowest return and highest risk)

| (IN US $) | RETURN-TO-RISK RATIO |
|---|---|
| 1.  U.S. Medical Equipment and Products | 27.4 |
| 2.  U.S. Semiconductor Industry | 20.9 |
| 3.  U.S. Instrumentation Industry | 17.8 |
| 4.  U.S. Information Technology | 13.0 |
| 5.  U.S. Comm. and Tel. Industry | 11.1 |
| 6.  Cdn. Telecommunications | 8.3 |
| 7.  U.S. Computer Industry | 8.1 |
| 8.  Korea | 5.1 |
| 9.  Cdn. Computer Industry | 2.2 |
| 10.  Cdn. Electronic Equipment | 1.9 |
| 11.  Singapore | 1.8 |
| 12.  Taiwan | 1.2 |
| 13.  Philippines | 1.0 |
| 14.  Malaysia | 0.9 |
| 15.  China | 0.7 |

Sources: International Monetary Fund, U.S. Department of Commerce,
Statistics Canada, and Nuala Beck & Associates Inc.

Many observers believe that China, like many other developing countries, is on a roll. People need basics, like shoes and cars and microwave ovens. But what good is it to invest hundreds of millions of dollars in a market when you are never sure you will break even?

Peugeot, the huge French automaker, has tried repeatedly to bail out of its Guanghou automotive facility, while to the north in Shenyang, GM's truck plant has sat idle for three years as GM attempts to decide what the plant should build. In addition, Volkswagen's Jettas are selling poorly in China. Chrysler Corp. executives, too, have abandoned their efforts to expand within China after battling knockoffs of their Jeeps made at its Beijing joint-venture facility.

If even half of the companies that have chased the global rainbow had looked beyond the allure of this Asian giant's growth and had calculated its volatility, they and their trusting shareholders would have realized that China's return-to-risk statistics make the country most unattractive as an investment. The table on page 71 shows how quickly the corresponding 15.7 volatility (or standard deviation) dampens China's five-year growth rate of 14.6 percent. Together these work out to a return-to-risk of only 0.9 percent. The newly installed electronic slot machines on long-haul British Airways flights to the Orient probably give better odds than the return-to-risk that business travellers face on the ground in China.

Right before our eyes, the long-term growth trend in these U.S. Four-Engine Industries is strengthening from a rate of 7.6 percent averaged over 10 years, to 9.3 percent averaged on a five-year basis, and to 9.6 percent on a one-year basis by 1996. Unlike China, Singapore, the Philippines, Malaysia, and other so-called growth markets, volatility in these Four-Engine Industries has historically been low, but continues to decline from a standard deviation average of 0.5 based on 10 years to 0.4 based on 5 years, to a steady 0.3 in 1996.

Now let's try pitting growth against volatility.

**As U.S. growth rises structurally ...**

### U.S. Four-Engine Growth (%)

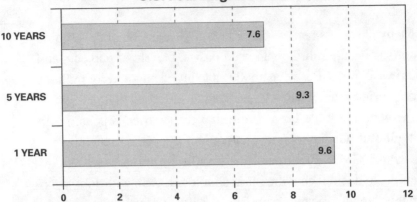

**... volatility is on the decline ...**

### U.S. Four-Engine Volatility (%)

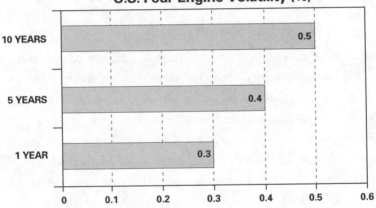

**... resulting in tremendously attractive returns compared to the risk involved.**

### U.S. Four-Engine Return-to-Risk (%)

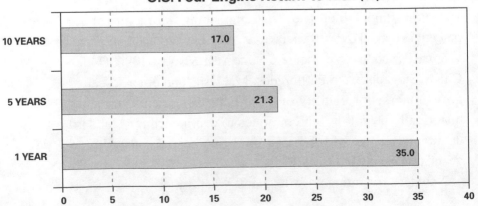

Sources: U.S. Department of Commerce, and Nuala Beck & Associates Inc.

The return-to-risk in Four-Engine Industries flies off the top of the scale, increasing from a coefficient of variation of 17.0 based on 10 years to 21.3 based on five, to a mouth-watering 35.0 in the last year.

The numbers demonstrate that a sweeping shift in the relative attractiveness of North America's fast-growing high-knowledge sector is under way now. Companies across this continent should leave off pursuing high-growth, low-return markets abroad and focus instead on developing high-growth, high-return markets that have been here all along.

## EAGER INDIANS AND THE MARKETING NIGHTMARE

When Bell Canada International set its sights on India's burgeoning middle class, they were dreaming delightful dreams. Notoriously inefficient, the subcontinent's local telephone market was backlogged with tens of millions of applicants all waiting patiently for installation of a simple telephone. What could be more promising than the prospect of introducing eager Indians to cellular phones, which offered great advantages over the old and rickety telephone system that hissed and crackled its way into the coming century?

There was a catch. Outside the very largest centres such as Bombay, Delhi, and Hyderabad, time isn't seen as money in India. Deeply engrained in everyday life in India is a conviction that if a telephone conversation cannot take place today, it can always take place tomorrow. Bell also discovered, much to its horror, that its Indian customers frequently preferred to search for pay phones to make calls when they were on the road, rather than use cell phones already in their cars; most Indians know that the government's income-tax collectors have taken to screening calls made over cellular networks. And there's more.

One story that has travelled within Bell Canada is how it took 12 frustrating months to get a straightforward permission to erect one cell site on one hilltop near the coastal community of Visakhapatnam. Bell Canada nearly went insane making the rounds of 19 government agencies — the state-run television network, the Indian navy, the lighthouse authority, to name a few — all to secure a few feet of access for itself atop a dusty hilltop.

Back in Canada, the demand for this everyday device has soared: this country now has more cell-phone subscribers than Germany and France have between them. Yet the corporate giant seems to have little regard for its customer base of knowledge workers. This should be, but doesn't appear to be, the focus of its corporate growth strategy.

## Jack's Story

Jack is your average well-heeled knowledge worker. Like most engineers, he has a short fuse when it comes to incompetence. He uses his cell phone, and needs it so he can stay in touch. We were instantly curious to hear what had happened when he showed up at our house on a Friday evening an hour late for dinner, with steam rising from both ears. He told us over a decent bottle of Merlot:

"I like dogs and children, but I'm fed up with seeing the advertisements for those mutt phones and from the rest of them in an industry that can't even deliver the product they're spending millions convincing me to buy.

"Customer service? No one could tell me when my phone would be available. They could tell me how to use each of the 78 buttons on it and how to e-mail my long-lost uncle in Lower Wherever, but not when I could actually take delivery of one.

"Meanwhile, businesses like mine are trying to incorporate the new technology to keep ourselves current and competitive, and here is the company selling the phones treating it like a giant video game. Altogether, I've waited five months for a dual-mode cell phone so I can stay connected if I move six inches outside the narrow analogue-phone corridor across Canada. Today was the last straw.

"Ron from head office called me today and said that my phone was available for pickup. After those long five months, I dropped everything at the office and headed to the kiosk at the mall where Ron told me my phone was waiting. I introduced myself to one of the very young customer-service associates, as they're called, and told him that Ron at head office had just called me to say my phone was ready.

"'Who's Ron?' came the reply.

"I explained about the priority list I'd been on for months and suggested that he check with his manager. Thirty minutes later he returned to where I had been standing patiently at the counter.

"'We don't have a priority list, sir. And we don't have any phones.'

"I suggested calmly that we call Ron at head office. Another 30 minutes later, the call got through and Ron at head office proceeded to train the kid over the phone on how the company's order-processing system worked. There is a priority list; I'm on it. But I still don't have a phone.

"Why? Because I now have to fill out a form that will allow them to do a personal credit check on me. I explain that my company is purchasing the phone, and I produce my corporate Visa card, but that simply won't do. I'm told that they are only allowed to process personal sales and credit checks at this location. 'We don't have any company forms here.'

"By this time, I've lost all patience. We get back on the phone to head office. I waited one and one-half hours on hold listening to Beethoven's Ninth Symphony — the whole thing. Every few minutes, a taped message came on, apologizing for the delay and telling me that I was important.

"Finally, a live person came on the line.

"A just-in-time training course was given to the customer-service associate, and he eventually produced the right form, which I duly filled out. I now have a phone number, a phone, and the promise that in two days, my phone will be activated by head office. They thanked me for my patience, and told me to have a 'nice' weekend."

It took my husband, Frank, and me the entire evening and several bottles of Merlot to convince Jack that he didn't really want to drown his phone in his wine or take it to the vet first thing Saturday morning to have it spayed.

# Virgin's Coming of Age

The upscale market of Singapore was a strategic nirvana for Virgin Retail Ltd., the major music-retail giant founded in the early 1970s by Sir Richard Branson, the ever-so-hip-and-tanned founder of Virgin Atlantic. When he isn't busy flying to his private island in the Caribbean, he sticks to his knitting — that is, he plans the expansion of his giant business empire. Singapore was his newest venture.

The company's feasibility study incorporated all the right buzzwords to hold the founder's attention. The economy of Singapore was waiting, ripe for expansion. The country's real gross national product was hot, hot, hot — average growth over five years, 16.7 percent, up slightly from 16.6 percent averaged over 10 years, and all in U.S. dollars. Its competitor, Tower Records, had secured prime retail space on the fourth floor of the upscale Pacific Plaza on Scotts Road. Not to be outdone, Virgin Records was seriously considering the newly vacated space of

Galéries Lafayette, the French retail department store giant, right at the junction of Orchard Road and Anguilla Park. The fact that Galéries Lafayette had to close its store should have rung alarm bells. It didn't. Virgin Records had big plans for its Asian mega-store venture. The grass seemed very green indeed, and mega-store planning was well in hand for Malaysia, Indonesia, Thailand, and the Philippines.

Fortunately, Virgin Records decided to take a second look before proceeding. Word came down from newly appointed executive Simon Burke that he was going to "revisit" the Asian project. No doubt he's very pleased he did. He was appalled to learn that competition in the market was cutthroat, the market was bouncing along, but about to head straight south. Luckily for him, he scrapped the plans at the right time. Within a year of the decision, the entire Asian economic miracle had collapsed. The dollar in Singapore was worth 26.3 percent less at year end 1997, and the local economy has tumbled from 7.8 percent real growth for that year to 2.5 percent in 1998 to date. Welcome to the world of volatility.

Despite the delectable growth rates of Singapore's economy for well over a decade, that growth rate's volatility became its Achilles heel, as it did for so many of Singapore's neighbours. Pitting Singapore's five-year growth rate of 16.7 percent against that rate's volatility of 6.4 knocked the country's return-to-risk all the way down to 2.6 percent.

Let's place these numbers in proper perspective. At 24.5 percent over five years, the return-to-risk for the U.S. information-tech-nology industry is almost 10 times higher than that of Singapore over the same timeframe. With a consumer base of 1.8 million employees in this sector, and 46 percent of these high-income knowledge workers with money to burn, you have a marketer's dream come true. Why chase an ephemeral global rainbow when these sectors right in the United States are almost three times larger than the entire economy of Singapore and larger than the economically and politically unstable Indonesia? With the wealth of many industries exceeding that of many nations, I'll opt for high-growth/low-risk markets in my own backyard any day.

## The Lions Are Coming, the Lions Are Coming

When Doug Ivester, Coca-Cola's chairman and chief executive officer, announced Coke's new corporate strategy, it was all I could do not to reach for an aspirin and down it with a big gulp of Pepsi.

Could Ivester be serious? Maybe it was just an "in" joke among the corporate set who meet in Davos, Switzerland, at each year's World Economic Summit. No one could begrudge them a little comic relief after the crushing meltdown of billions of dollars' worth of their company's precious capital in the Asian financial collapse.

Now Coke is talking up the merits of investing in Africa? To my amazement, all the pat phrases came flooding out: The continent is "too large to ignore"; so is Antarctica, I thought, but size alone doesn't mean you have to invest in frozen wasteland. "Africa is changing for the better...." Sure it is, but you don't have to invest in a quagmire of corruption and instability just for the sake of collecting frequent-flyer miles.

Do some companies never learn? No wonder globalization as we know it is giving way to a very different world economy — perhaps nothing short of a total reengineering of global economic strategy is what is required, if only to minimize the reliance of some companies on their own blind faith in the mantra of globalization.

# 4

# THE GROWTH SURPRISE

## North America's Growth Elite

As I mentioned in a previous chapter, 38 industries in North America have been growing faster than the hottest emerging economies. Some names on the list of what I call North America's Growth Elite are familiar. Naturally, industries such as those that produce semiconductors top the charts. In the United States alone, that industry surpasses in revenues the entire gross domestic product of Greece.

What each of the 38 have in common is that their return-to-risk, the growth-versus-volatility measurement that I described in Chapter 3, *is higher than the return-to-risk the Asia economies averaged* in the glory days when they set the world afire as the fastest growing economies on Earth and before their recent collapse. Note that the cutoff point used in the tables and graphs on the following pages is 1996, the year before the economies of Asia nosedived. (Consequently, comparisons could also be drawn between the performance of North America's fastest growing industries and that of the emerging economies in their heyday. Even the diehard optimists who convince themselves that Asia's collapse is just a flesh wound will have to acknowledge that these North American industries beat the Asian miracle any day.)

Each industry also tells a unique story of technological change, growth, and prosperity and is fodder for some of the most telling case studies of flexibility and ingenuity. If you are a little taken aback to see the U.S. furniture industry on the list of this growth elite, consider how this old industry has transformed itself completely again, through its widespread use of new technology and the individual companies' concerted effort to market themselves and their products aggressively to the new breed of knowledge workers in North America.

After taking a terrible beating through the 1980s, the companies that survived — such as Thomasville and Ethan Allen — had no choice but to modernize their operations on a massive scale. They introduced new furniture lines and designs to appeal to today's well-off knowledge worker. Check out Thomasville's Web site at www.thomasville.com or browse through Ethan Allen's appealing catalogue of fine furnishings; the days when knowledge workers furnished their bachelor apartments in "Early Boxcrate" have given way to the drop-dead designer loft in Toronto or the beautifully furnished million-dollar homes in Palo Alto, California, in what has blossomed into more than an enclave of nerds with no taste. The 42 million knowledge workers of America have become an economic force in their own right. They have the incomes, the job security, and the consumer confidence to single-handedly demand that whole industries revamp their whole businesses. Ethan Allen devotes entire pages of its catalogue to beautifully crafted computer work centres, for example, in a variety of fine wood veneers. Yessir, today's knowledge worker has come a long way from the $75 computer desk that came in your choice of white or black laminated plywood.

The industries powering North America's growth surprise and our future prosperity aren't limited to this list of the Growth Elite. A new kind of knowledge is pushing growth in ways completely new to humankind.

## North America's Growth Elite

### UNITED STATES

1. Communication Equipment, excluding defense
2. Electronics & Electrical Equipment
3. Com. & Tel. Equipment
4. Computer & Office Equipment
5. Semiconductor & Electronic Components
6. Medical Equipment & Supplies
7. Instrumentation
8. Medical Instruments & Supplies
9. Ophthalmic Goods, Watches & Clocks
10. Information Technology
11. Agricultural Chemicals
12. Construction & Mining Equipment
13. Industrial Machinery
14. Metalworking Machinery
15. Cutlery & Handtools
16. Transformers, Switchgears & Switchboards
17. Travel Trailers & Campers
18. Wood Buildings & Mobile Homes
19. Lubricating Oils & Greases
20. Household Furniture
21. Petroleum & Coal Products
22. Misc. Manufacturing Industries
23. Misc. Personal Goods

### CANADA

1. Electrical & Electronic Products
2. Communication
3. Telecommunication Carriers
4. Banks & Credit Unions
5. Truck Transport
6. Business Services
7. Educational Services
8. Wood Preservation, Particle & Wafer Board
9. Primary Metals
10. Machine Shops
11. Hardware, Tool and Cutlery
12. Rubber Products
13. Plastic Products
14. Motor Vehicle Parts & Accessories
15. Plastic & Synthetic Resin

Sources: U.S. Department of Commerce, Statistics Canada

83

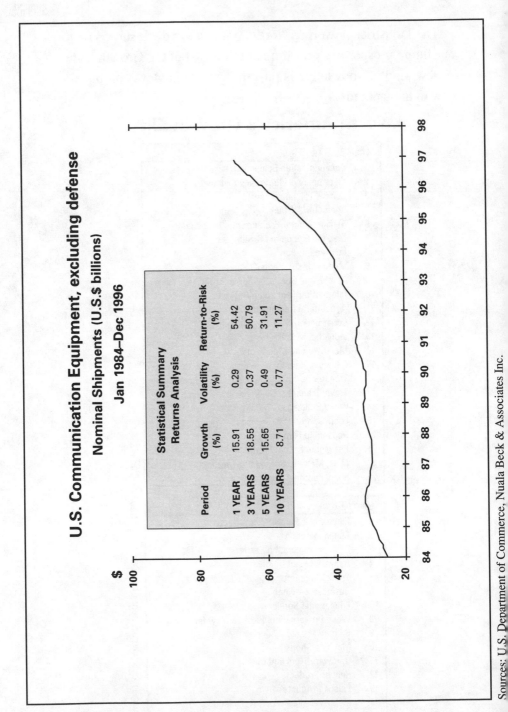

# U.S. Communication Equipment, excluding defense

## Nominal Shipments (U.S.$ billions)

### Jan 1984–Dec 1996

**Statistical Summary
Returns Analysis**

| Period | Growth (%) | Volatility (%) | Return-to-Risk (%) |
|--------|-----------|----------------|---------------------|
| 1 YEAR | 15.91 | 0.29 | 54.42 |
| 3 YEARS | 18.55 | 0.37 | 50.79 |
| 5 YEARS | 15.65 | 0.49 | 31.91 |
| 10 YEARS | 8.71 | 0.77 | 11.27 |

Sources: U.S. Department of Commerce, Nuala Beck & Associates Inc.

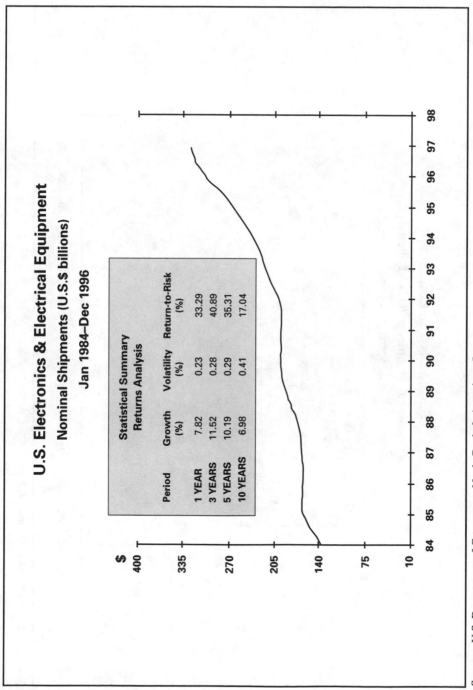

# U.S. Electronics & Electrical Equipment

## Nominal Shipments (U.S.$ billions)

### Jan 1984–Dec 1996

**Statistical Summary**
**Returns Analysis**

| Period | Growth (%) | Volatility (%) | Return-to-Risk (%) |
|---|---|---|---|
| 1 YEAR | 7.82 | 0.23 | 33.29 |
| 3 YEARS | 11.52 | 0.28 | 40.89 |
| 5 YEARS | 10.19 | 0.29 | 35.31 |
| 10 YEARS | 6.98 | 0.41 | 17.04 |

Sources: U.S. Department of Commerce, Nuala Beck & Associates Inc.

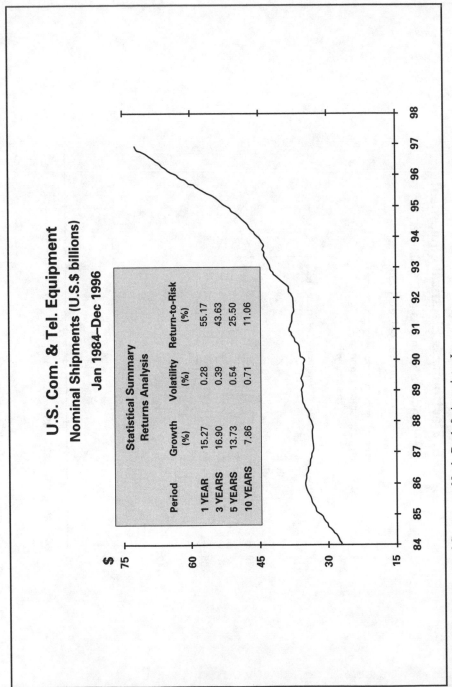

## U.S. Com. & Tel. Equipment
### Nominal Shipments (U.S.$ billions)
### Jan 1984–Dec 1996

**Statistical Summary**
**Returns Analysis**

| Period | Growth (%) | Volatility (%) | Return-to-Risk (%) |
|--------|-----------|----------------|--------------------|
| 1 YEAR | 15.27 | 0.28 | 55.17 |
| 3 YEARS | 16.90 | 0.39 | 43.63 |
| 5 YEARS | 13.73 | 0.54 | 25.50 |
| 10 YEARS | 7.86 | 0.71 | 11.06 |

Sources: U.S. Department of Commerce, Nuala Beck & Associates Inc.

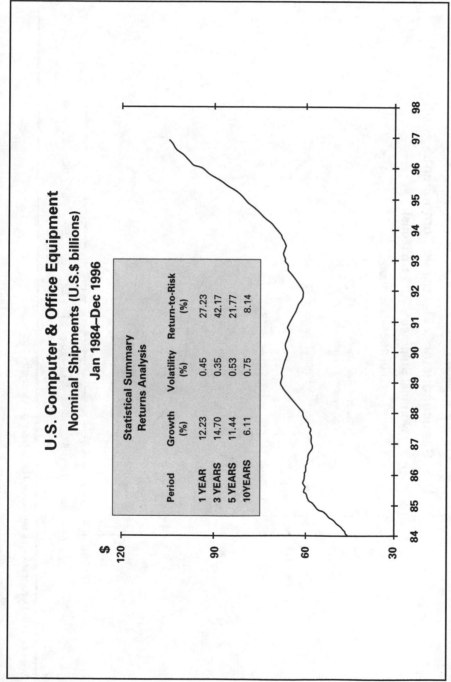

## U.S. Computer & Office Equipment

### Nominal Shipments (U.S.$ billions)

### Jan 1984–Dec 1996

**Statistical Summary Returns Analysis**

| Period | Growth (%) | Volatility (%) | Return-to-Risk (%) |
|--------|-----------|----------------|--------------------|
| 1 YEAR | 12.23 | 0.45 | 27.23 |
| 3 YEARS | 14.70 | 0.35 | 42.17 |
| 5 YEARS | 11.44 | 0.53 | 21.77 |
| 10 YEARS | 6.11 | 0.75 | 8.14 |

Sources: U.S. Department of Commerce, Nuala Beck & Associates Inc.

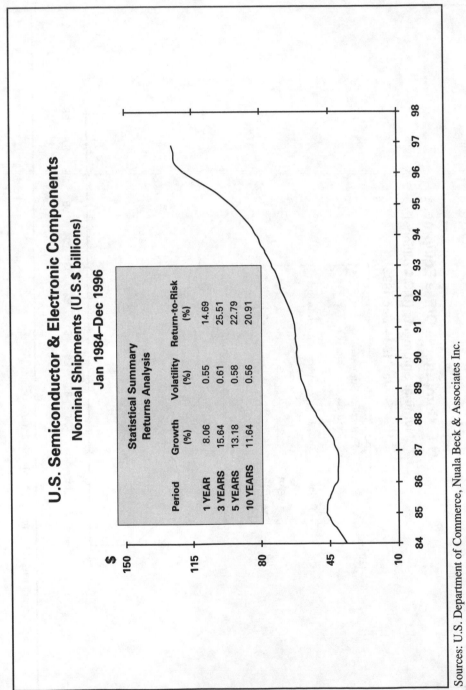

# U.S. Semiconductor & Electronic Components

## Nominal Shipments (U.S.$ billions)

### Jan 1984–Dec 1996

**Statistical Summary**
**Returns Analysis**

| Period | Growth (%) | Volatility (%) | Return-to-Risk (%) |
|---|---|---|---|
| 1 YEAR | 8.06 | 0.55 | 14.69 |
| 3 YEARS | 15.64 | 0.61 | 25.51 |
| 5 YEARS | 13.18 | 0.58 | 22.79 |
| 10 YEARS | 11.64 | 0.56 | 20.91 |

Sources: U.S. Department of Commerce, Nuala Beck & Associates Inc.

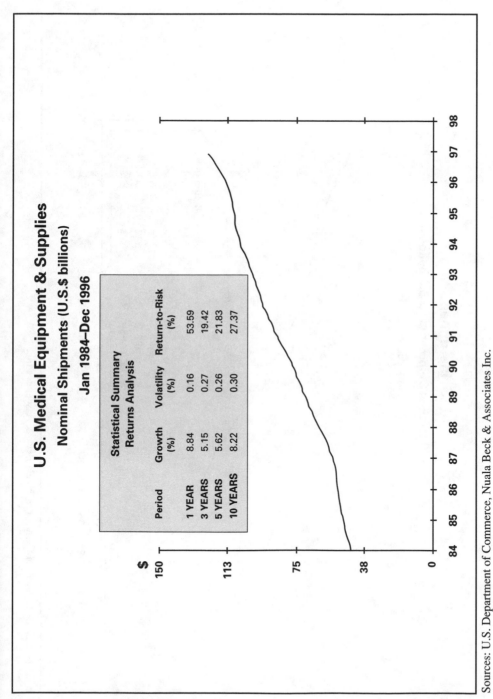

## U.S. Medical Equipment & Supplies

### Nominal Shipments (U.S.$ billions)

### Jan 1984–Dec 1996

**Statistical Summary**
**Returns Analysis**

| Period | Growth (%) | Volatility (%) | Return-to-Risk (%) |
|--------|-----------|----------------|--------------------|
| 1 YEAR | 8.84 | 0.16 | 53.59 |
| 3 YEARS | 5.15 | 0.27 | 19.42 |
| 5 YEARS | 5.62 | 0.26 | 21.83 |
| 10 YEARS | 8.22 | 0.30 | 27.37 |

Sources: U.S. Department of Commerce, Nuala Beck & Associates Inc.

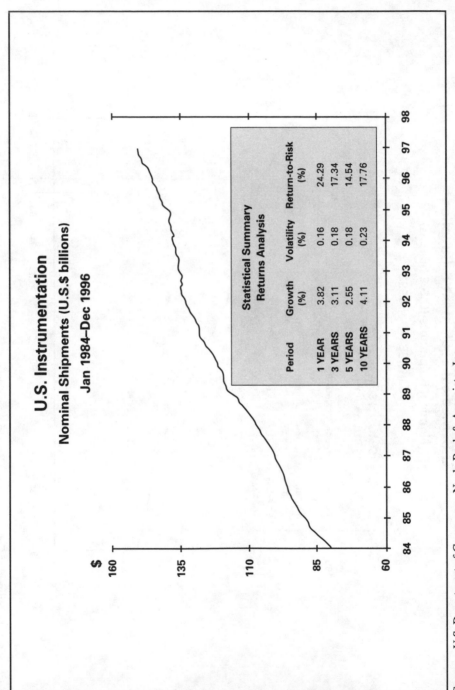

## U.S. Instrumentation
### Nominal Shipments (U.S.$ billions)
### Jan 1984–Dec 1996

**Statistical Summary**
**Returns Analysis**

| Period | Growth (%) | Volatility (%) | Return-to-Risk (%) |
|---|---|---|---|
| 1 YEAR | 3.82 | 0.16 | 24.29 |
| 3 YEARS | 3.11 | 0.18 | 17.34 |
| 5 YEARS | 2.55 | 0.18 | 14.54 |
| 10 YEARS | 4.11 | 0.23 | 17.76 |

Sources: U.S. Department of Commerce, Nuala Beck & Associates Inc.

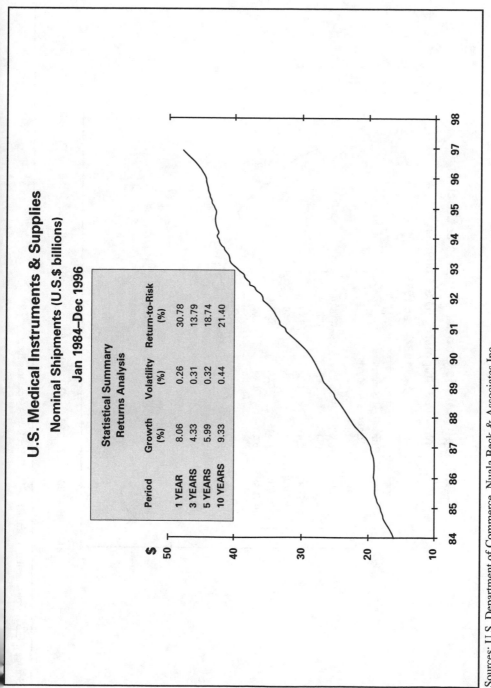

## U.S. Medical Instruments & Supplies

### Nominal Shipments (U.S.$ billions)
### Jan 1984–Dec 1996

**Statistical Summary**
**Returns Analysis**

| Period | Growth (%) | Volatility (%) | Return-to-Risk (%) |
|--------|-----------|----------------|--------------------|
| 1 YEAR | 8.06 | 0.26 | 30.78 |
| 3 YEARS | 4.33 | 0.31 | 13.79 |
| 5 YEARS | 5.99 | 0.32 | 18.74 |
| 10 YEARS | 9.33 | 0.44 | 21.40 |

Sources: U.S. Department of Commerce, Nuala Beck & Associates Inc.

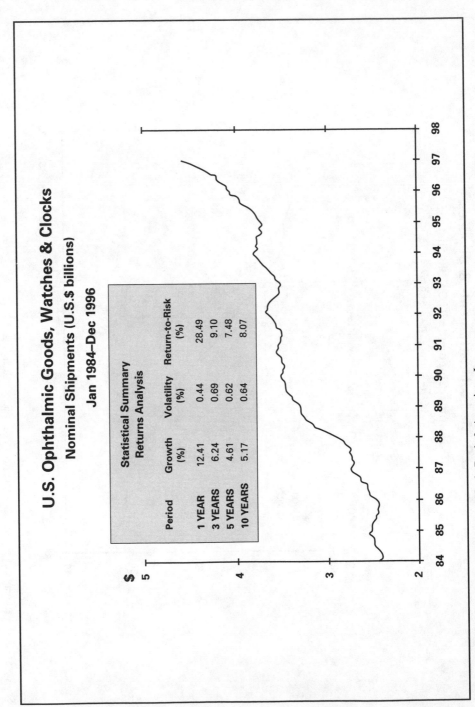

# U.S. Ophthalmic Goods, Watches & Clocks

**Nominal Shipments (U.S.$ billions)**

**Jan 1984–Dec 1996**

### Statistical Summary
### Returns Analysis

| Period | Growth (%) | Volatility (%) | Return-to-Risk (%) |
|--------|-----------|---------------|-------------------|
| 1 YEAR | 12.41 | 0.44 | 28.49 |
| 3 YEARS | 6.24 | 0.69 | 9.10 |
| 5 YEARS | 4.61 | 0.62 | 7.48 |
| 10 YEARS | 5.17 | 0.64 | 8.07 |

Sources: U.S. Department of Commerce, Nuala Beck & Associates Inc.

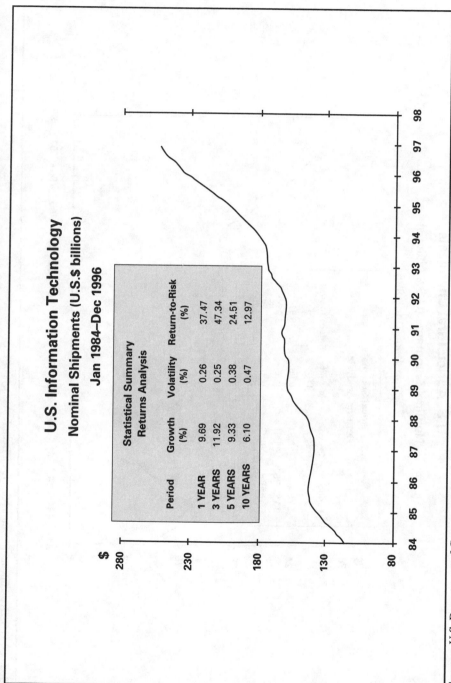

## U.S. Information Technology
### Nominal Shipments (U.S.$ billions)
### Jan 1984–Dec 1996

Statistical Summary
Returns Analysis

| Period | Growth (%) | Volatility (%) | Return-to-Risk (%) |
|---|---|---|---|
| 1 YEAR | 9.69 | 0.26 | 37.47 |
| 3 YEARS | 11.92 | 0.25 | 47.34 |
| 5 YEARS | 9.33 | 0.38 | 24.51 |
| 10 YEARS | 6.10 | 0.47 | 12.97 |

Sources: U.S. Department of Commerce, Nuala Beck & Associates Inc.

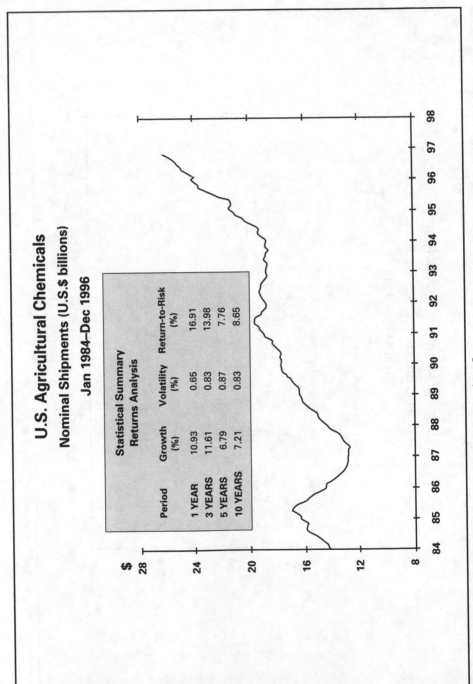

## U.S. Agricultural Chemicals
### Nominal Shipments (U.S.$ billions)
### Jan 1984–Dec 1996

**Statistical Summary**
**Returns Analysis**

| Period | Growth (%) | Volatility (%) | Return-to-Risk (%) |
|---|---|---|---|
| 1 YEAR | 10.93 | 0.65 | 16.91 |
| 3 YEARS | 11.61 | 0.83 | 13.98 |
| 5 YEARS | 6.79 | 0.87 | 7.76 |
| 10 YEARS | 7.21 | 0.83 | 8.65 |

Sources: U.S. Department of Commerce, Nuala Beck & Associates Inc.

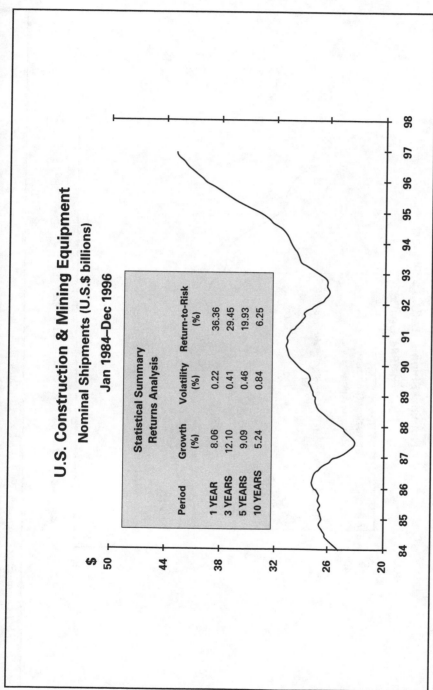

## U.S. Construction & Mining Equipment
### Nominal Shipments (U.S.$ billions)
### Jan 1984–Dec 1996

**Statistical Summary**
**Returns Analysis**

| Period | Growth (%) | Volatility (%) | Return-to-Risk (%) |
|---|---|---|---|
| 1 YEAR | 8.06 | 0.22 | 36.36 |
| 3 YEARS | 12.10 | 0.41 | 29.45 |
| 5 YEARS | 9.09 | 0.46 | 19.93 |
| 10 YEARS | 5.24 | 0.84 | 6.25 |

Sources: U.S. Department of Commerce, Nuala Beck & Associates Inc.

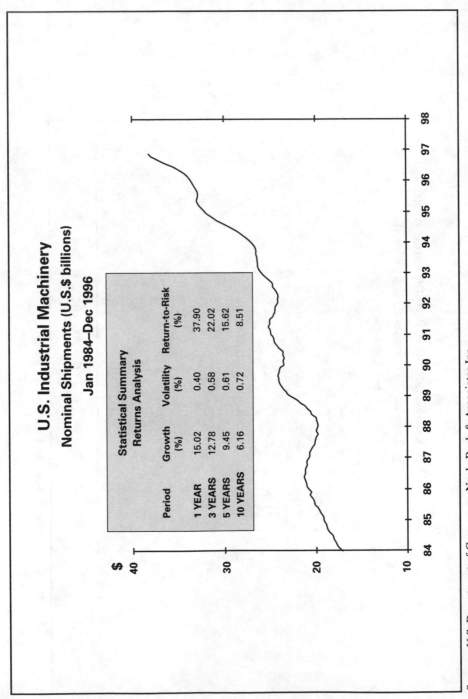

## U.S. Industrial Machinery
### Nominal Shipments (U.S.$ billions)
### Jan 1984–Dec 1996

**Statistical Summary**
**Returns Analysis**

| Period | Growth (%) | Volatility (%) | Return-to-Risk (%) |
|---|---|---|---|
| 1 YEAR | 15.02 | 0.40 | 37.90 |
| 3 YEARS | 12.78 | 0.58 | 22.02 |
| 5 YEARS | 9.45 | 0.61 | 15.62 |
| 10 YEARS | 6.16 | 0.72 | 8.51 |

Sources: U.S. Department of Commerce, Nuala Beck & Associates Inc.

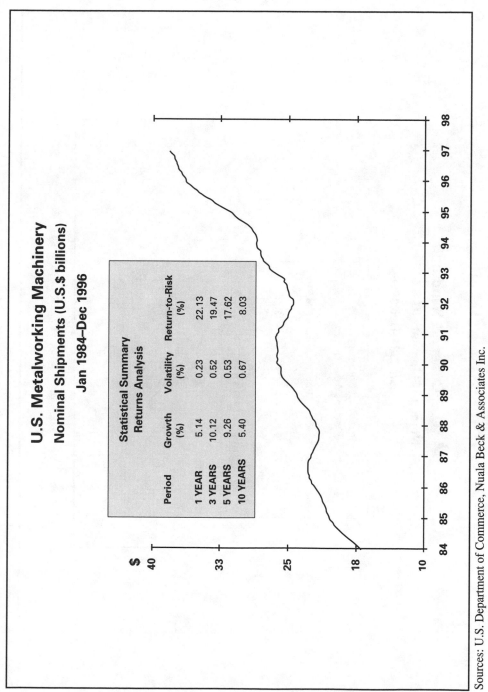

U.S. Metalworking Machinery
Nominal Shipments (U.S.$ billions)
Jan 1984–Dec 1996

Statistical Summary
Returns Analysis

| Period | Growth (%) | Volatility (%) | Return-to-Risk (%) |
|---|---|---|---|
| 1 YEAR | 5.14 | 0.23 | 22.13 |
| 3 YEARS | 10.12 | 0.52 | 19.47 |
| 5 YEARS | 9.26 | 0.53 | 17.62 |
| 10 YEARS | 5.40 | 0.67 | 8.03 |

Sources: U.S. Department of Commerce, Nuala Beck & Associates Inc.

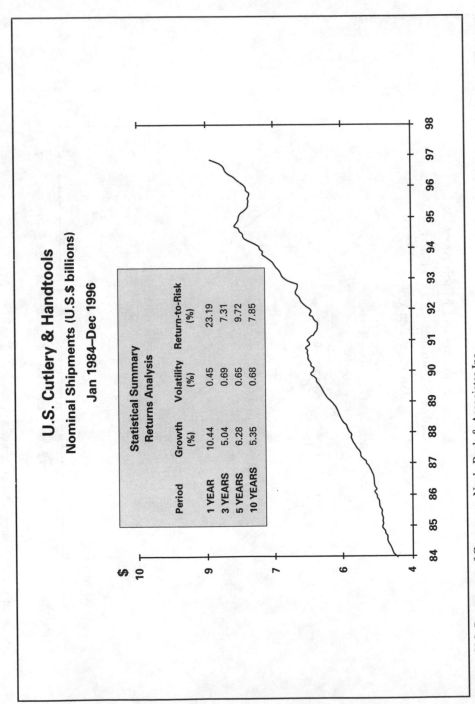

## U.S. Cutlery & Handtools
### Nominal Shipments (U.S.$ billions)
### Jan 1984–Dec 1996

**Statistical Summary**
**Returns Analysis**

| Period | Growth (%) | Volatility (%) | Return-to-Risk (%) |
|---|---|---|---|
| 1 YEAR | 10.44 | 0.45 | 23.19 |
| 3 YEARS | 5.04 | 0.69 | 7.31 |
| 5 YEARS | 6.28 | 0.65 | 9.72 |
| 10 YEARS | 5.35 | 0.68 | 7.85 |

Sources: U.S. Department of Commerce, Nuala Beck & Associates Inc.

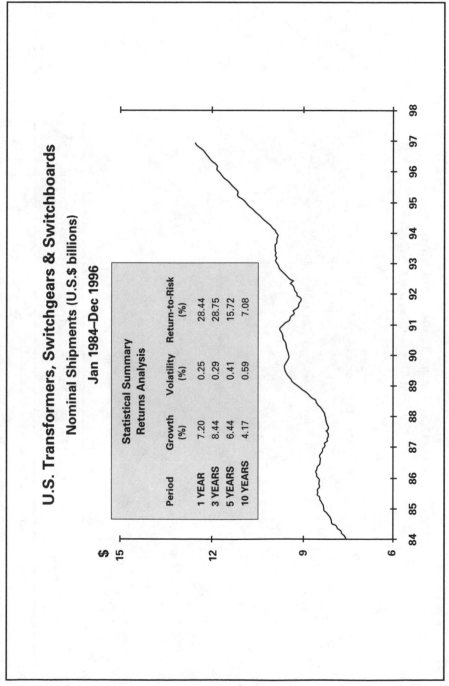

## U.S. Transformers, Switchgears & Switchboards

### Nominal Shipments (U.S.$ billions)

### Jan 1984–Dec 1996

| Statistical Summary Returns Analysis | | | |
|---|---|---|---|
| Period | Growth (%) | Volatility (%) | Return-to-Risk (%) |
| 1 YEAR | 7.20 | 0.25 | 28.44 |
| 3 YEARS | 8.44 | 0.29 | 28.75 |
| 5 YEARS | 6.44 | 0.41 | 15.72 |
| 10 YEARS | 4.17 | 0.59 | 7.08 |

Sources: U.S. Department of Commerce, Nuala Beck & Associates Inc.

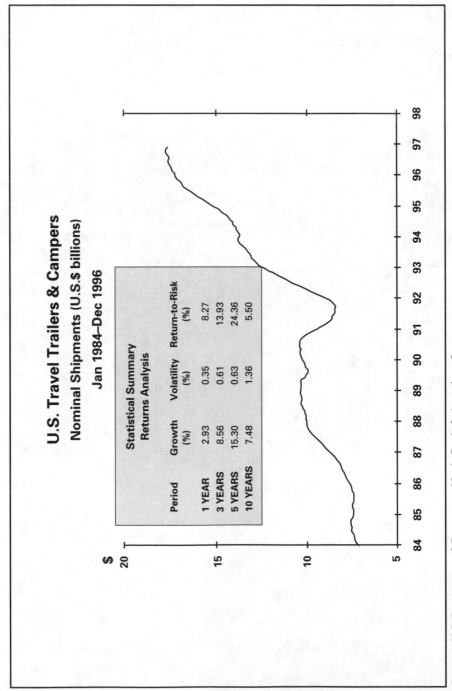

## U.S. Travel Trailers & Campers
### Nominal Shipments (U.S.$ billions)
### Jan 1984–Dec 1996

**Statistical Summary**
**Returns Analysis**

| Period | Growth (%) | Volatility (%) | Return-to-Risk (%) |
|---|---|---|---|
| 1 YEAR | 2.93 | 0.35 | 8.27 |
| 3 YEARS | 8.56 | 0.61 | 13.93 |
| 5 YEARS | 15.30 | 0.63 | 24.36 |
| 10 YEARS | 7.48 | 1.36 | 5.50 |

Sources: U.S. Department of Commerce, Nuala Beck & Associates Inc.

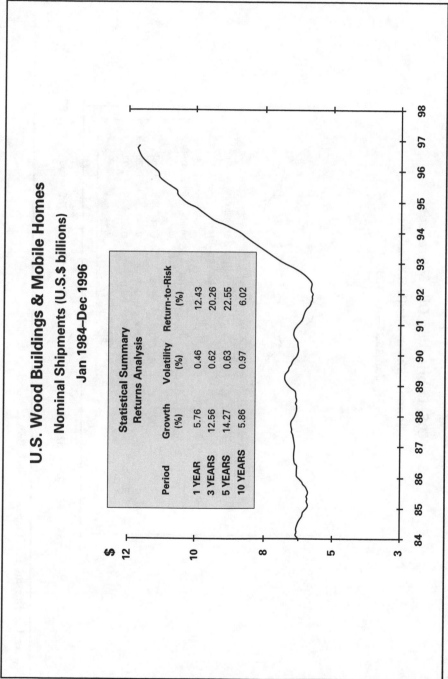

# U.S. Wood Buildings & Mobile Homes
### Nominal Shipments (U.S.$ billions)
### Jan 1984–Dec 1996

**Statistical Summary**
**Returns Analysis**

| Period | Growth (%) | Volatility (%) | Return-to-Risk (%) |
|--------|-----------|----------------|---------------------|
| 1 YEAR | 5.76 | 0.46 | 12.43 |
| 3 YEARS | 12.56 | 0.62 | 20.26 |
| 5 YEARS | 14.27 | 0.63 | 22.55 |
| 10 YEARS | 5.86 | 0.97 | 6.02 |

Sources: U.S. Department of Commerce, Nuala Beck & Associates Inc.

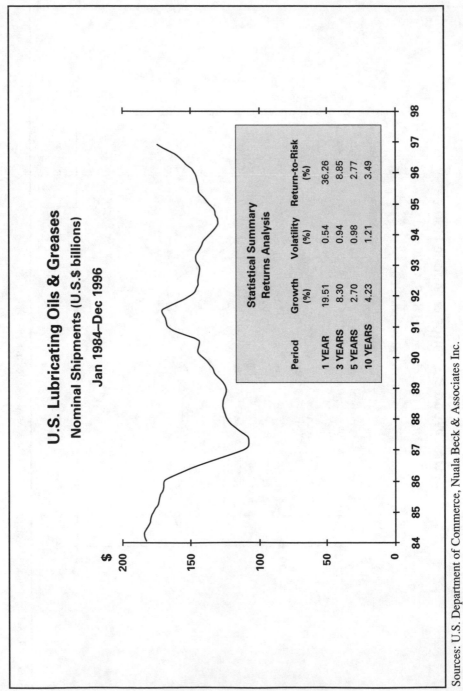

## U.S. Lubricating Oils & Greases
### Nominal Shipments (U.S.$ billions)
### Jan 1984–Dec 1996

**Statistical Summary**
**Returns Analysis**

| Period | Growth (%) | Volatility (%) | Return-to-Risk (%) |
|---|---|---|---|
| 1 YEAR | 19.51 | 0.54 | 36.26 |
| 3 YEARS | 8.30 | 0.94 | 8.85 |
| 5 YEARS | 2.70 | 0.98 | 2.77 |
| 10 YEARS | 4.23 | 1.21 | 3.49 |

Sources: U.S. Department of Commerce, Nuala Beck & Associates Inc.

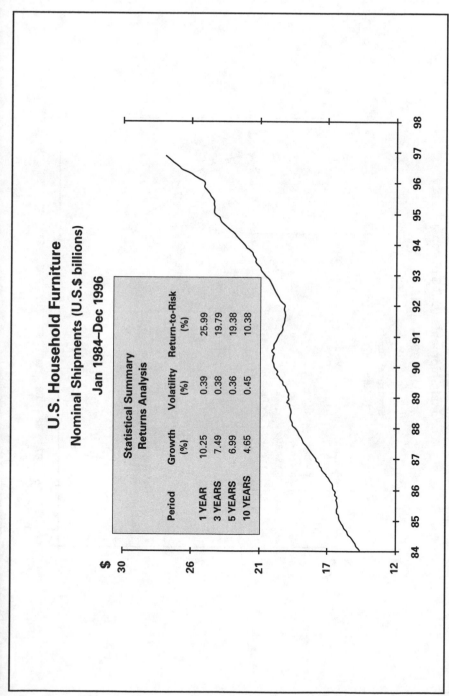

## U.S. Household Furniture

### Nominal Shipments (U.S.$ billions)

### Jan 1984–Dec 1996

**Statistical Summary**
**Returns Analysis**

| Period | Growth (%) | Volatility (%) | Return-to-Risk (%) |
|---|---|---|---|
| 1 YEAR | 10.25 | 0.39 | 25.99 |
| 3 YEARS | 7.49 | 0.38 | 19.79 |
| 5 YEARS | 6.99 | 0.36 | 19.38 |
| 10 YEARS | 4.65 | 0.45 | 10.38 |

Sources: U.S. Department of Commerce, Nuala Beck & Associates Inc.

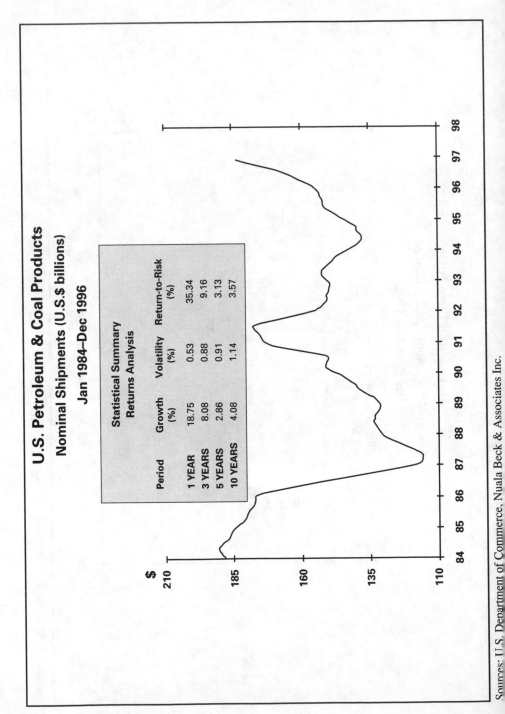

## U.S. Petroleum & Coal Products
### Nominal Shipments (U.S.$ billions)
### Jan 1984–Dec 1996

**Statistical Summary
Returns Analysis**

| Period | Growth (%) | Volatility (%) | Return-to-Risk (%) |
|--------|-----------|----------------|--------------------|
| 1 YEAR | 18.75 | 0.53 | 35.34 |
| 3 YEARS | 8.08 | 0.88 | 9.16 |
| 5 YEARS | 2.86 | 0.91 | 3.13 |
| 10 YEARS | 4.08 | 1.14 | 3.57 |

Sources: U.S. Department of Commerce, Nuala Beck & Associates Inc.

104

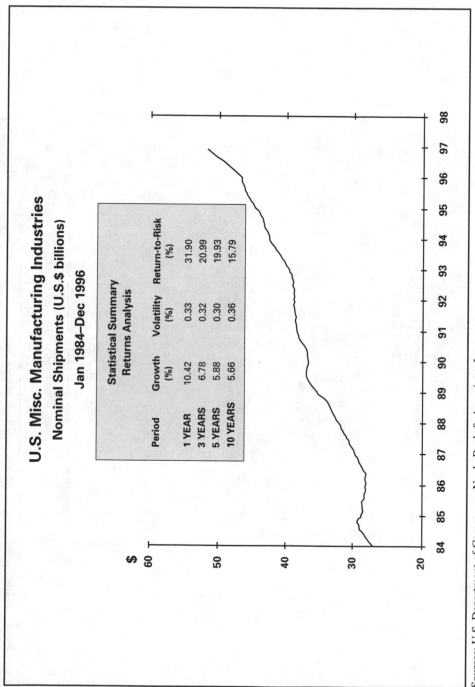

## U.S. Misc. Manufacturing Industries
### Nominal Shipments (U.S.$ billions)
### Jan 1984–Dec 1996

**Statistical Summary**
**Returns Analysis**

| Period | Growth (%) | Volatility (%) | Return-to-Risk (%) |
|--------|-----------|----------------|--------------------|
| 1 YEAR | 10.42 | 0.33 | 31.90 |
| 3 YEARS | 6.78 | 0.32 | 20.99 |
| 5 YEARS | 5.88 | 0.30 | 19.93 |
| 10 YEARS | 5.66 | 0.36 | 15.79 |

Sources: U.S. Department of Commerce, Nuala Beck & Associates Inc.

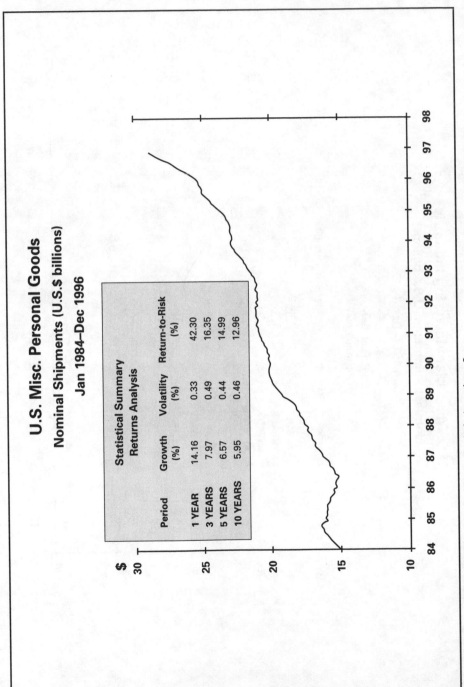

## U.S. Misc. Personal Goods
### Nominal Shipments (U.S.$ billions)
### Jan 1984–Dec 1996

**Statistical Summary Returns Analysis**

| Period | Growth (%) | Volatility (%) | Return-to-Risk (%) |
|--------|-----------|----------------|---------------------|
| 1 YEAR | 14.16 | 0.33 | 42.30 |
| 3 YEARS | 7.97 | 0.49 | 16.35 |
| 5 YEARS | 6.57 | 0.44 | 14.99 |
| 10 YEARS | 5.95 | 0.46 | 12.96 |

Sources: U.S. Department of Commerce, Nuala Beck & Associates Inc.

106

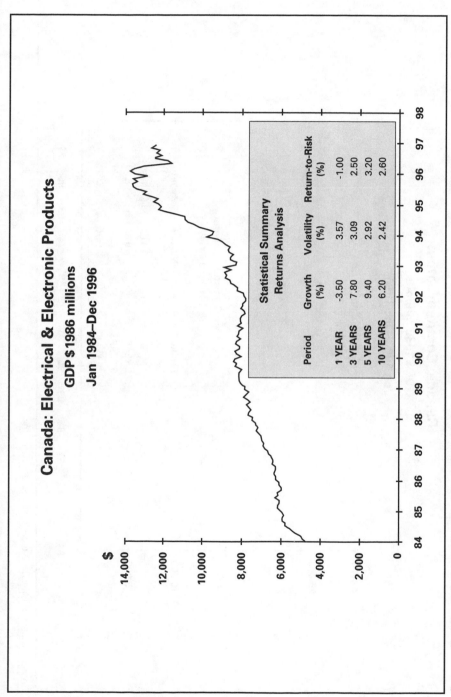

# Canada: Electrical & Electronic Products

## GDP $1986 millions

## Jan 1984–Dec 1996

### Statistical Summary
### Returns Analysis

| Period | Growth (%) | Volatility (%) | Return-to-Risk (%) |
|---|---|---|---|
| 1 YEAR | -3.50 | 3.57 | -1.00 |
| 3 YEARS | 7.80 | 3.09 | 2.50 |
| 5 YEARS | 9.40 | 2.92 | 3.20 |
| 10 YEARS | 6.20 | 2.42 | 2.60 |

Sources: Statistics Canada, Nuala Beck & Associates Inc.

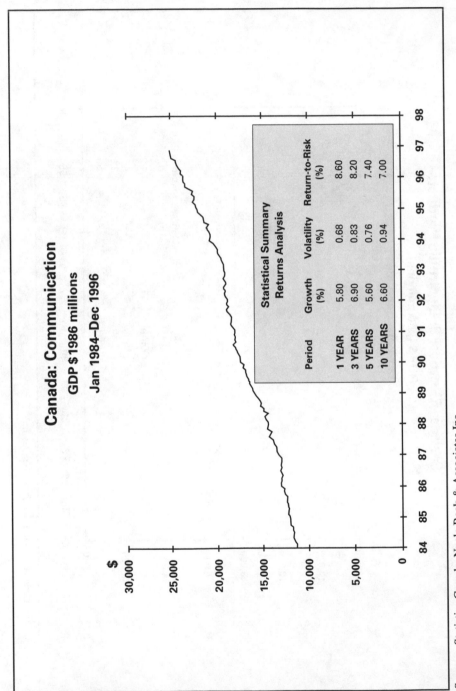

## Canada: Communication
### GDP $1986 millions
### Jan 1984–Dec 1996

**Statistical Summary
Returns Analysis**

| Period | Growth (%) | Volatility (%) | Return-to-Risk (%) |
|---|---|---|---|
| 1 YEAR | 5.80 | 0.68 | 8.60 |
| 3 YEARS | 6.90 | 0.83 | 8.20 |
| 5 YEARS | 5.60 | 0.76 | 7.40 |
| 10 YEARS | 6.60 | 0.94 | 7.00 |

Sources: Statistics Canada, Nuala Beck & Associates Inc.

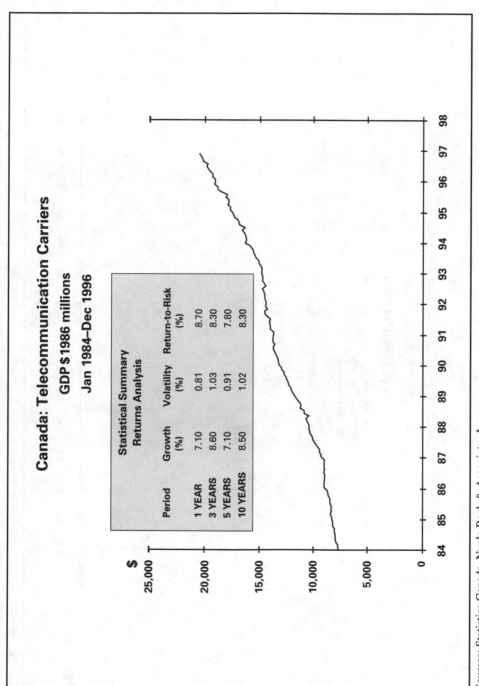

## Canada: Telecommunication Carriers

### GDP $ 1986 millions

### Jan 1984–Dec 1996

| Statistical Summary Returns Analysis | | | |
|---|---|---|---|
| Period | Growth (%) | Volatility (%) | Return-to-Risk (%) |
| 1 YEAR | 7.10 | 0.81 | 8.70 |
| 3 YEARS | 8.60 | 1.03 | 8.30 |
| 5 YEARS | 7.10 | 0.91 | 7.80 |
| 10 YEARS | 8.50 | 1.02 | 8.30 |

Sources: Statistics Canada, Nuala Beck & Associates Inc.

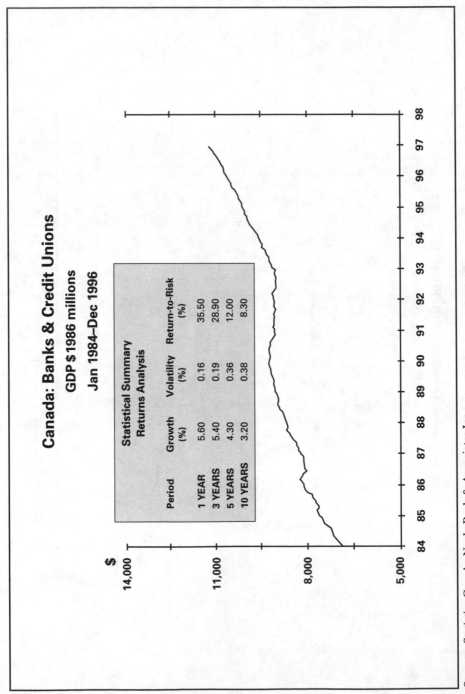

# Canada: Banks & Credit Unions

## GDP $1986 millions

### Jan 1984–Dec 1996

**Statistical Summary**
**Returns Analysis**

| Period | Growth (%) | Volatility (%) | Return-to-Risk (%) |
|---|---|---|---|
| 1 YEAR | 5.60 | 0.16 | 35.50 |
| 3 YEARS | 5.40 | 0.19 | 28.90 |
| 5 YEARS | 4.30 | 0.36 | 12.00 |
| 10 YEARS | 3.20 | 0.38 | 8.30 |

Sources: Statistics Canada, Nuala Beck & Associates Inc.

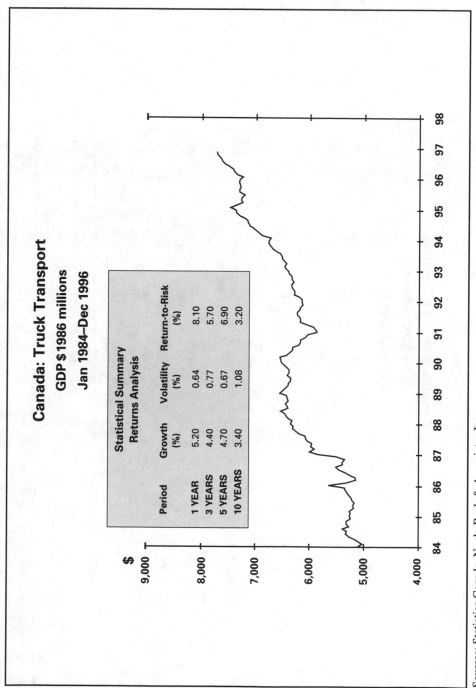

**Canada: Truck Transport**

GDP $ 1986 millions

Jan 1984–Dec 1996

| Statistical Summary Returns Analysis | | | |
|---|---|---|---|
| Period | Growth (%) | Volatility (%) | Return-to-Risk (%) |
| 1 YEAR | 5.20 | 0.64 | 8.10 |
| 3 YEARS | 4.40 | 0.77 | 5.70 |
| 5 YEARS | 4.70 | 0.67 | 6.90 |
| 10 YEARS | 3.40 | 1.08 | 3.20 |

Sources: Statistics Canada, Nuala Beck & Associates Inc.

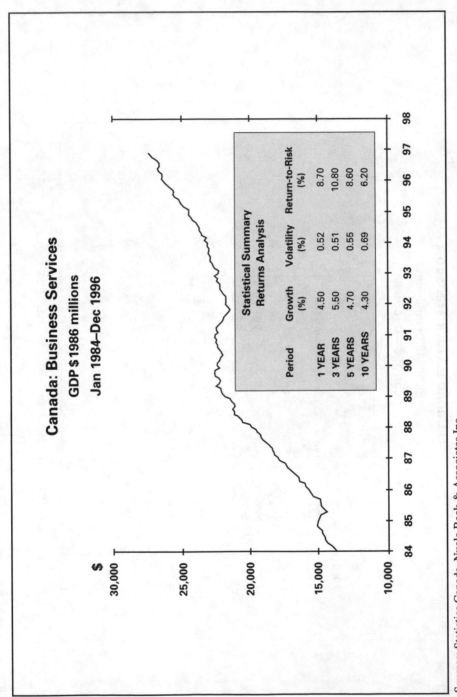

## Canada: Business Services
### GDP $ 1986 millions
### Jan 1984–Dec 1996

**Statistical Summary**
**Returns Analysis**

| Period | Growth (%) | Volatility (%) | Return-to-Risk (%) |
|---|---|---|---|
| 1 YEAR | 4.50 | 0.52 | 8.70 |
| 3 YEARS | 5.50 | 0.51 | 10.80 |
| 5 YEARS | 4.70 | 0.55 | 8.60 |
| 10 YEARS | 4.30 | 0.69 | 6.20 |

Sources: Statistics Canada, Nuala Beck & Associates Inc.

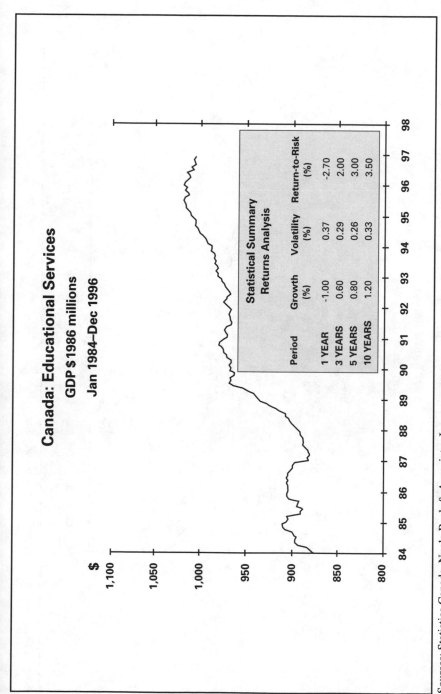

## Canada: Educational Services

**GDP $ 1986 millions**

**Jan 1984–Dec 1996**

### Statistical Summary
### Returns Analysis

| Period | Growth (%) | Volatility (%) | Return-to-Risk (%) |
|---|---|---|---|
| 1 YEAR | -1.00 | 0.37 | -2.70 |
| 3 YEARS | 0.60 | 0.29 | 2.00 |
| 5 YEARS | 0.80 | 0.26 | 3.00 |
| 10 YEARS | 1.20 | 0.33 | 3.50 |

Sources: Statistics Canada, Nuala Beck & Associates Inc.

113

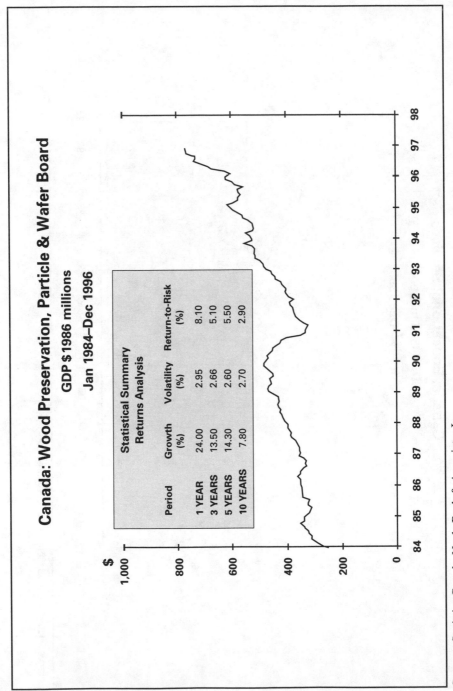

# Canada: Wood Preservation, Particle & Wafer Board

### GDP $ 1986 millions
### Jan 1984–Dec 1996

**Statistical Summary**
**Returns Analysis**

| Period | Growth (%) | Volatility (%) | Return-to-Risk (%) |
|---|---|---|---|
| 1 YEAR | 24.00 | 2.95 | 8.10 |
| 3 YEARS | 13.50 | 2.66 | 5.10 |
| 5 YEARS | 14.30 | 2.60 | 5.50 |
| 10 YEARS | 7.80 | 2.70 | 2.90 |

Sources: Statistics Canada, Nuala Beck & Associates Inc.

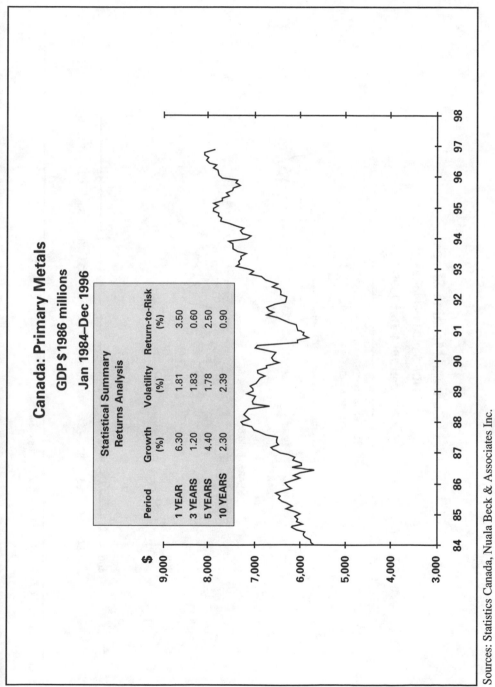

Canada: Primary Metals
GDP $1986 millions
Jan 1984–Dec 1996

| Period | Statistical Summary Returns Analysis | | |
|---|---|---|---|
| | Growth (%) | Volatility (%) | Return-to-Risk (%) |
| 1 YEAR | 6.30 | 1.81 | 3.50 |
| 3 YEARS | 1.20 | 1.83 | 0.60 |
| 5 YEARS | 4.40 | 1.78 | 2.50 |
| 10 YEARS | 2.30 | 2.39 | 0.90 |

Sources: Statistics Canada, Nuala Beck & Associates Inc.

115

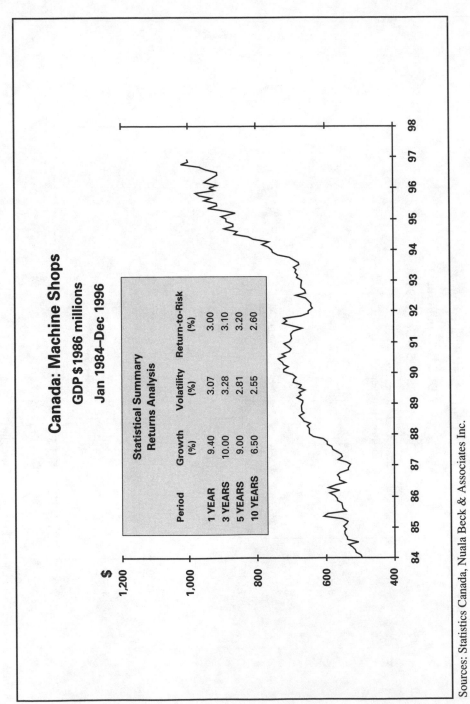

## Canada: Machine Shops
### GDP $ 1986 millions
### Jan 1984–Dec 1996

**Statistical Summary
Returns Analysis**

| Period | Growth (%) | Volatility (%) | Return-to-Risk (%) |
|--------|-----------|----------------|---------------------|
| 1 YEAR | 9.40 | 3.07 | 3.00 |
| 3 YEARS | 10.00 | 3.28 | 3.10 |
| 5 YEARS | 9.00 | 2.81 | 3.20 |
| 10 YEARS | 6.50 | 2.55 | 2.60 |

Sources: Statistics Canada, Nuala Beck & Associates Inc.

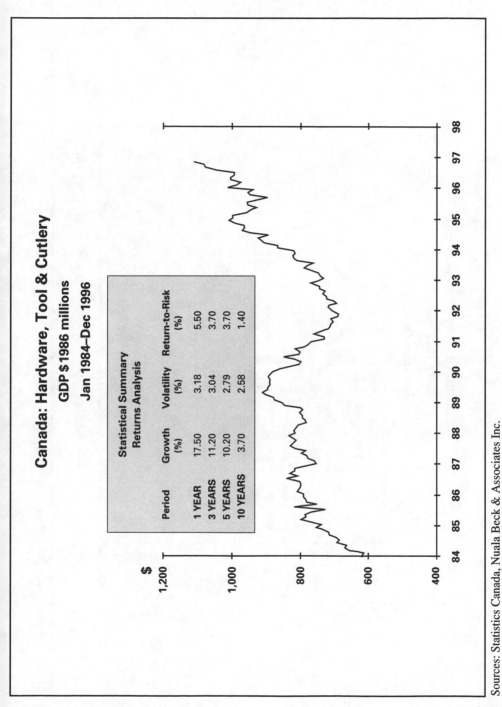

# Canada: Hardware, Tool & Cutlery

**GDP $1986 millions**

**Jan 1984–Dec 1996**

### Statistical Summary
### Returns Analysis

| Period | Growth (%) | Volatility (%) | Return-to-Risk (%) |
|--------|------------|----------------|---------------------|
| 1 YEAR | 17.50 | 3.18 | 5.50 |
| 3 YEARS | 11.20 | 3.04 | 3.70 |
| 5 YEARS | 10.20 | 2.79 | 3.70 |
| 10 YEARS | 3.70 | 2.58 | 1.40 |

Sources: Statistics Canada, Nuala Beck & Associates Inc.

117

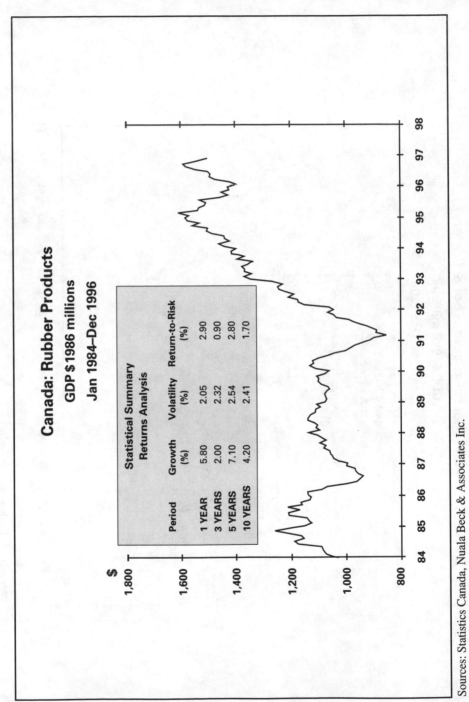

Canada: Rubber Products

GDP $ 1986 millions

Jan 1984–Dec 1996

**Statistical Summary**
**Returns Analysis**

| Period | Growth (%) | Volatility (%) | Return-to-Risk (%) |
|---|---|---|---|
| 1 YEAR | 5.80 | 2.05 | 2.90 |
| 3 YEARS | 2.00 | 2.32 | 0.90 |
| 5 YEARS | 7.10 | 2.54 | 2.80 |
| 10 YEARS | 4.20 | 2.41 | 1.70 |

Sources: Statistics Canada, Nuala Beck & Associates Inc.

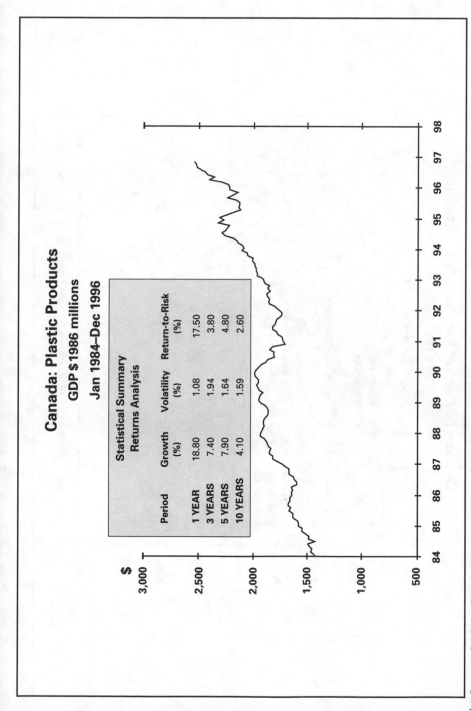

# Canada: Plastic Products

## GDP $ 1986 millions

## Jan 1984–Dec 1996

| Statistical Summary Returns Analysis | | | |
|---|---|---|---|
| Period | Growth (%) | Volatility (%) | Return-to-Risk (%) |
| 1 YEAR | 18.80 | 1.08 | 17.50 |
| 3 YEARS | 7.40 | 1.94 | 3.80 |
| 5 YEARS | 7.90 | 1.64 | 4.80 |
| 10 YEARS | 4.10 | 1.59 | 2.60 |

Sources: Statistics Canada, Nuala Beck & Associates Inc.

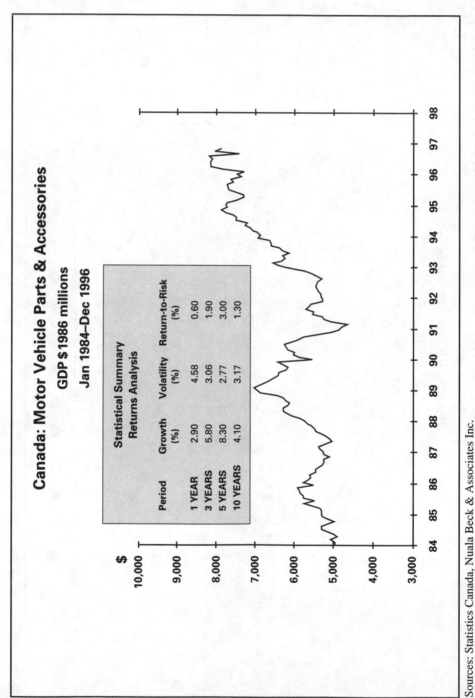

# Canada: Motor Vehicle Parts & Accessories

**GDP $ 1986 millions**

**Jan 1984–Dec 1996**

### Statistical Summary
### Returns Analysis

| Period | Growth (%) | Volatility (%) | Return-to-Risk (%) |
|---|---|---|---|
| 1 YEAR | 2.90 | 4.58 | 0.60 |
| 3 YEARS | 5.80 | 3.06 | 1.90 |
| 5 YEARS | 8.30 | 2.77 | 3.00 |
| 10 YEARS | 4.10 | 3.17 | 1.30 |

Sources: Statistics Canada, Nuala Beck & Associates Inc.

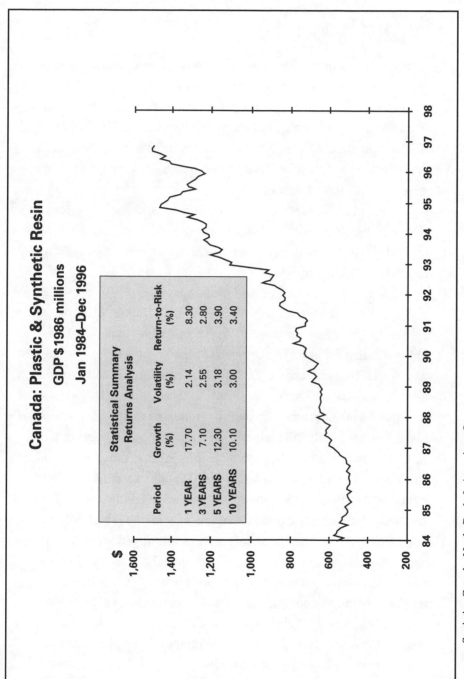

# Canada: Plastic & Synthetic Resin

### GDP $ 1986 millions

### Jan 1984–Dec 1996

**Statistical Summary
Returns Analysis**

| Period | Growth (%) | Volatility (%) | Return-to-Risk (%) |
|---|---|---|---|
| 1 YEAR | 17.70 | 2.14 | 8.30 |
| 3 YEARS | 7.10 | 2.55 | 2.80 |
| 5 YEARS | 12.30 | 3.18 | 3.90 |
| 10 YEARS | 10.10 | 3.00 | 3.40 |

Sources: Statistics Canada, Nuala Beck & Associates Inc.

# Knowledge Paradigms

Every new economy has a unique knowledge base that distinguishes it from the one that preceded it. This was as true of Britain's Industrial Revolution as it was of this century's mass manufacturing era dominated by the United States. Similarly, the knowledge base of this New Economy is changing Canada's economic and financial future profoundly — more so than anyone could have foreseen.

In the last decade, my consulting firm spearheaded a series of major research projects. Through these we identified what we termed the New Economy, a term which our firm subsequently registered as a trademark.

We began with a detailed and exciting study of 207 industries in the United States and a further 269 industries in Canada, as shown by the chart on page 125. The facts revealed that new industries had replaced old ones as the economy's major engines of growth. This process we explained as economic evolution. We also identified the New Economy's "Four Engines" — also discussed in the previous chapter — industries particularly well placed strategically and already so large that they generated further growth beyond their own sectors. At that time, the world still referred to information technology, medical technology, and many other kinds of technology as "emerging industries." Our research data demonstrated to what extent they had already assumed this role. They were larger, they employed more people, and they packed more economic punch than the traditional industries of autos and housing that supported a strong Canadian economy a generation ago. And these same industries, broken down into their component corporations, also showed us through the statistics that they reflected a very different knowledge base from any other in the history of humankind.

Take a long look at the explosive increase in the knowledge

base of today's economy. It's more than double that of Canada's economy of the past. This quantum leap hints at the astounding changes still to be made to the very fabric of our society, and to how the global economy will evolve and function. More important, it provides a tantalizing sense of the possibilities lying ahead for our civilization.

## Average Knowledge Ratio (%) of Each Era

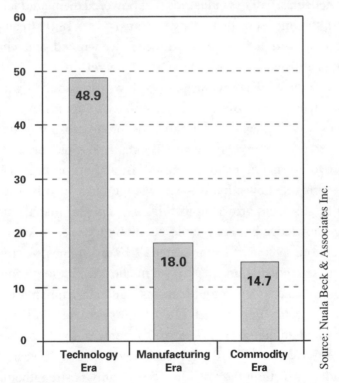

Source: Nuala Beck & Associates Inc.

The knowledge base of the twenty-first century's economy already averages 48.9 knowledge workers per 100 people employed. This astonishing change marks the growing divide between the New Economy of the late 20th century and the average knowledge base of 18.0 knowledge workers per 100 people employed in the major, traditional industries most of this century.

Consider the changes that the world has gone through since the

Industrial Revolution. From education standards to social values, from entertainment and medicine to technology — virtually every part of our society has been affected by this rising knowledge base. This has meant a quantum leap in our standard of living as well.

From a knowledge base of 14.7 (using 1997 data on knowledge ratios) for the engines that drove the industries of the nineteenth-century's Industrial Revolution to 18.0, the average such knowledge base of the industries that powered the manufacturing world, the impact of that change, from 14.7 to 18.0 affected the fundamentals of how we worked, where we worked, and what we worked at. And we haven't seen anything yet.

The graph on the previous page follows the astounding leap in the knowledge base of this New Economy's engines. As impressive as it is, it does not show the enormous prosperity that the knowledge economy will eventually make possible for us. That's why every Canadian should see the first chart on page 126. In stark terms it shows that this knowledge base, as driven by the Four Engines, has grown almost *five times higher* than the underlying knowledge base of the old economy we used to know.

Between 1986 and 1996, Canada's Four Engines — computers and semiconductors; health and medical technology; communications and telecommunications; and instrumentation — turned in a dazzling growth rate of 73.6 percent. This meant a compound annual growth rate of 5.7 percent — almost double Canada's overall real GDP growth rate of the last 20 years. And Canada's growth in the knowledge economy is strengthening in terms of its very infrastructure: last year these engines positively roared, with a growth rate of 8.6 percent.

Compared to mass manufacturing, which generated real growth of only 15.9 percent — today's is 73.6 percent — you can understand why it is a very reasonable bet to look forward to great prosperity in the twenty-first century. The worldwide recession that we are now tipping into won't last forever.

# Knowledge Paradigms

## 1880–1918

### Commodity-Driven Era

**Average Knowledge Ratio of Four Engines**
14.7%

**Free Education**
Elementary school

**Key Factor**
Cheap steel

**Four Engines**
Textiles, coal, steel, and railroads

**Infrastructure**
Railroads, shipping and telegraph

**Leading Economic Indicators**
Pig iron production, Railroad operating income, inner tube production, coal and coke production, textile mill production, cotton consumption

## 1918–1981

### Manufacturing-Driven Era

**Average Knowledge Ratio of Four Engines**
18.0%

**Free Education**
High school

**Key Factor**
Cheap energy, especially oil

**Four Engines**
Autos, machine tools, housing, retailing

**Infrastructure**
Highways, airports, telephone

**Leading Economic Indicators**
Industrial production, capacity utilization, machine tool orders, retail sales, housing starts, auto sales

## 1981–2035

### Technology-Driven Era

**Average Knowledge Ratio of Four Engines**
48.9%

**Free Education**
College and university is already free in Ireland. It is only a matter of time before other countries, including Canada, feel the pressure to keep pace.

**Key Factor**
Cheap chips (microchips)

**Four Engines**
Computers and semiconductors, health and medical technology, communication and telecommunication, instrumentation

**Infrastructure**
Telecommunications satellites, fibre optics, LANs and WANs

**Leading Economic Indicators**
Computer production, semiconductor production, instrumentation sales, high-tech trade balance, knowledge employment, medical starts

Source: Nuala Beck & Associates Inc.

## Canada's 10-Year Growth
### (% change from 10 years ago)

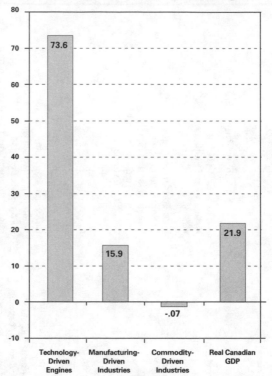

Sources: Statistics Canada, Nuala Beck & Associates Inc.

## Canada's Average Annual Growth
## Rates for the Last 10 years (%)

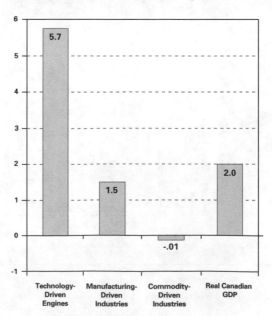

Sources: Statistics Canada, Nuala Beck & Associates Inc.

# Education's Growth Dividend

Look beyond the engines that are driving the knowledge economy and you will discover, as we did, that they lead a fairly impressive pack overall. In total, our research has identified almost 40 high-knowledge industries across Canada, each generating its own momentum and wealth.

In 1996, these high-knowledge industries accounted for 22.7 percent of Canada's gross domestic product. By 1997, they had grown to a whopping 30.9 percent of the country's economic output.

One look at the knowledge base of today's economy proves how vital a third-level education is already for every Canadian. Just as a high school education eventually became a basic requirement over the last 50 years, and Britain's Industrial Revolution led to grade-school education and the basic skills in reading and writing a century earlier, now I predict it won't be long before a university or community-college education (already a universal necessity of life) therefore becomes a universal right in every knowledge-based economy, including Canada's. Countries that establish the universality of a third-level education the fastest, such as the examples I've cited several times of Ireland and the Netherlands, are already reaping enormous dividends in the form of growth over those countries that adhere to the educational standards of a world that no longer exists.

# Canada's Knowledge Intensity 1997

### The Knowledge Intensity of
### Canada's Economic Output
### (% of real GDP)

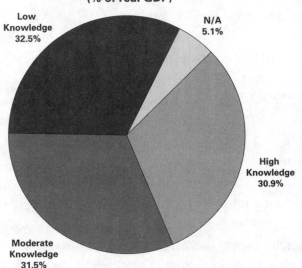

Low Knowledge 32.5%

N/A 5.1%

High Knowledge 30.9%

Moderate Knowledge 31.5%

# Canada's High-Knowledge Industries

Accounting & Legal Services

Advertising Services

Agricultural Chemicals

Aircraft & Aircraft Parts

Architectural & Scientific Services

Banks

Cable Television

Chemical Products

Computer Equipment

Computer Services

Consumer Electronics

Credit Unions

Education

Electronic Equipment

Electronic Parts & Components

Financial Intermediaries

Government Services
(includes Provincial, Federal,
& Local)

Health & Social Services

Industrial Inorganic Chemicals

Industrial Organic Chemicals

Instrumentation

Membership Organizations

Motion Picture & Video Production &
Distribution

Pharmaceutical & Medicine

Radio & TV Broadcasting

Soap & Cleaning Compounds

Telecommunication Equipment

Toilet Preparations

Sources: Statistics Canada, Nuala Beck & Associates Inc.

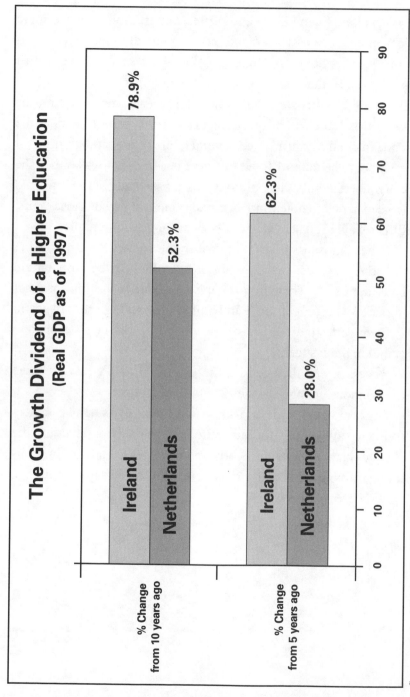

**The Growth Dividend of a Higher Education**
(Real GDP as of 1997)

% Change
from 10 years ago

Ireland — 78.9%
Netherlands — 52.3%

% Change
from 5 years ago

Ireland — 62.3%
Netherlands — 28.0%

Sources: Ireland Central Statistics Office, Netherlands Central Bureau of Statistics

Okay, okay, I can hear some professors grumbling at the mere idea of all those first-year students clogging their hallowed academic halls. A Southern Ontario biology professor told me, with a straight face, that her 15 hours of teaching per week was a full-time job! She insisted that although she had been teaching the same first- and second-year science courses for 12 years at the same institution, she needed several hours of preparation time for each hour she taught! I had to figure her problem was either she could not remember her Biology 101, or she had not remembered to keep her class notes and lecture outlines for any of those years. Either way, I felt she was totally out of touch with reality.

Other dinosaurs doubtless lurk in the bushes, too, muttering that free university and community-college education would bankrupt us all. They are probably the same old clump of reactionaries who fought tooth and nail to prevent high schools from throwing open their doors to any young Canadian who wished to attend in the last century.

Access to and the need for higher education are just one area of enormous change for the twenty-first century.

For companies large and small and for all of us baby boomers trying to save money for our retirement years, understanding the changes happening to our world and what lies ahead will bring us immeasurable rewards. Frankly, not to accept the challenge would be unthinkable.

# 5

# THE DECLINE OF GLOBALIZATION AS WE KNOW IT

## GLOBALIZATION AS IMPERIALISM

Until the end of the First World War, globalization and impe-rialism went hand in hand; Europe's rulers had long carved up global markets into colonies and traded them back and forth among themselves as siblings exchange Park Place for Board-walk in a heated game of Monopoly today.

But did the captains of industry and government recognize the beginning of the end of globalization as they knew it as the First World War swept over the face of Europe? Such prescience seems unlikely. Some of the most profound changes creep up on us when we are least expecting them, and in the midst of the chaos of global war people concerned themselves more with surviving than with predicting future economic trends.

# The Global Vacuum of 1918–1945

The imperial version of globalization ended abruptly in 1918. It took until 1945 to fill the resulting vacuum caused by war and destruction with a new and vastly different form of globalization. Recuperating, Europe looked inward, its energies absorbed by the wholesale rebuilding of its war-torn economies, a devastating decline in its populations, hyperinflation, and depression. Meanwhile, the United States turned its considerable technological prowess, given furious impetus by its production for the war effort, to developing its new mass-manufacturing economy into a global powerhouse.

Today, Old Europe — Germany, France, Italy, Austria, Belgium, and Sweden — is focusing inward as it did then, striving to protect old interests and old industries. At the same time, New Europe — the Netherlands, Ireland, Britain, and most of Nordic Europe — is concentrating on playing larger roles in the knowledge economy. North America has already established itself as *the* technological powerhouse in this rapidly unfolding global vacuum which I am about to describe.

# Globalization and the Great "Isms" of the Twentieth Century

In the aftermath of the Second World War, the United States assumed the lead in restructuring the world's economy. In the last few decades, Canada has been moving tentatively to fill a leadership role itself within this U.S.-dominated world economy.

From the postwar period through the 1980s, globalization came to mean a world divided between two superpowers, each of which divvied up world markets into those based on the free,

capitalist model and those run on the centrally planned communist model. Thus economic globalization clearly demarcated the
great "isms" of this century.

International organizations presided over the capitalist world
market — the United Nations, the International Monetary Fund,
the World Bank — which was governed by such multilateral
agreements as the General Agreement of Tariffs and Trade
(GATT). Essentially parallel organizations — presided over the
communist economies of the world.

Did whole economies, companies large or small, or investors
really anticipate such changes in the balance of world economic
power? Did they see the writing on the wall? Could they see far
enough to recognize that such a different world order of philoso-
phies, economic and political, of new "isms," would move in to
fill the vacuum the Second World War left at its end? And when
the Berlin Wall came tumbling down, didn't we all stare in
wonder that capitalism had prevailed?

# GLOBALIZATION AS INTERNATIONAL COOPERATION

The Soviet Empire dissolved before our eyes between 1985 and
1991, flashing yet another new definition of "global" across the
economic landscape of the world. Such groups as the G-7,
OECD, the United Nations, the International Monetary Fund,
and the many other world organizations that sprang to life this
century eagerly spearheaded a move towards what they termed
international cooperation. Now, they had a *real* purpose: to
manage the *entire* world.

These organizations deftly handled various international
crises, such as the stock market crash of 1987, and the economic
meltdowns of entire countries, such as Mexico's collapse in
1994. Such institutional successes gave rise to hopes that this

latest incarnation of globalization, the late-twentieth-century "managing partnership," would prove both secure and sustainable. For a decade it actually appeared to be working. By early 1997, a generalized, comfortable faith in this arrangement seemed almost palpable worldwide. Then, in June 1997, the Thai baht went kaput, triggering the current Asia crisis. There will be no easy escape from its far-reaching effects.

At first many observers interpreted the crisis as a short-term blip. Economists, analysts, and journalists alike presumed that the world's managing partners could move quickly to restore any lost confidence, much as a corporation's board of directors aim to do on what used to be a smaller scale. They'd fix the problem, and the region's rate of economic growth would return to normal. Why, Asia Pacific might even emerge the better for it, just as Mexico had done.

Little did anyone realize as the Asian economic crisis deepened that it spelled the beginning of the death throes of twentieth-century globalization.

# The Great Divide

What happens to cooperation and partnership, any partnership, when an organization's most senior executives begin to recognize deep and irreconcilable differences among themselves? In terms of current conditions, what kind of future can we expect for the forces of globalization, defined as international cooperation, when the members of the G-7 countries move apart, each to pursue fundamentally dissimilar goals and visions? At the moment we are still in the early days of answering this enormous question.

The powerful and prestigious G-7 countries include Canada, the United States, Britain, Germany, France, Italy, and Japan. Russia would skin a bear to join this elite group, but the members have insisted Russia sit on the sidelines until it can demonstrate that it can manage its own economy and collect the taxes that its own companies and individuals so deftly avoid paying. The Russian republic is in no position to dole out advice to others, when it can't even manage its own economy. So far, the former Soviet Union is lucky to be allowed to attend the meetings as an observer, given the financial disaster and massive economic collapse the country is going through in 1998.

For the past 23 years, the G-7 has functioned as the executive committee of the global economy, even while its members have been drifting further and further apart in the 1990s. Influenced by the growth model of the United States, Canada, and the United Kingdom, along with such non-G-7 members as Ireland, the Netherlands, Singapore, Denmark, Finland, Norway, and Iceland, have boldly restructured themselves for the new knowledge economy. They have steadily raised their competitive positions in the world at the expense of those countries that have not revamped their economies in the same way.

On the other side of the G-7 table, Japan, France, Italy, and Germany are permitting their once formidable competitive positions to wither and die. Japan has sunk to 9th place in global competitiveness, France to 19th place, Italy to 34th, and the historically powerful German economy has plunged to 14th most competitive world economy. This ranks it well beneath Finland and Denmark. Labour unions in Germany remain inflexible. Management remains leery of change. Governments, short on vision themselves, react to change when confronted with it but seem incapable of initiating and therefore controlling it. Within the membership of the G-7, countries have become very strange bedfellows with one another. They no longer share the same values or vision — vital preconditions if they are to work towards the future together.

**135**

# The Decline of Globalization as We Know It

In Chapter 2, I cited two advantages that set Canada ahead of most other countries: flexibility and transparency. The lack of these same strengths gnaws away at the old globalization today. The absence of the former impedes rapid change, and the absence of the latter puts the protection of vested interests ahead of economic progress. Both are fracturing relations between the G-7 members. If such tensions continue to worsen, the current approach to managing the global economy will become utterly unworkable within a decade.

Japan, France, Italy, and Germany are not the first countries in history to face economic atrophy. Nor will they be the last. As far back as you care to go in history, great economic and financial empires have dwindled and died by letting slip their leads in the global economies of their days. Like the great Austrian or British empires of the nineteenth century, economic powers in the world have survived and eventually declined while living off the glories of their past success for as long as possible. Eventually each has seen its economic power dissipate and has exited from the world stage.

Japan in particular will remember 1998 as the year of its great recession, the year when its economy was humbled before all the world. Most of the banks in the land of the rising sun are broke today. Their bad debts, estimated at a staggering US$700 billion, exceed Canada's entire gross domestic product. Brokerage-house chairmen take to window-ledges rather than face the public humiliation of accepting life-saving mergers as the weaker partners. Meanwhile, the Bank of Japan and the Ministry of Finance argue bitterly over whether to admit the truth about Japan's mounting bank losses, which have greatly worsened as its neighbours' economies have collapsed as well. Trying to shore up bad domestic-loan portfolios by lending recklessly to developing neighbours is not, as Martha Stewart might say, "a good thing."

Don't count on Japan to be an engine fuelling the knowledge economy. Rather than contributing leadership and vision, the nation has actually injected serious tension and fragmentation into the G-7. The country holds an important position as the Asian economic engine for growth. Clearly it has failed to carry out this role. Meanwhile, the country watches a stream of prime ministers passing through revolving doors, each tinkering with minor economic stimuli rather than embarking on the major restructuring the nation desperately needs. The government must challenge old and deeply vested interests. To date its politicians and business leaders have chosen to ride out a slow and agonizing decline rather than make hard decisions.

France, Italy, and Germany are marching only steps behind Japan. France and Italy, to put it delicately, have economies that are less than transparent. As discussed in Chapter 2, the levels of corruption in business, benignly if not overtly supported by their politicians, provide a less than desirable model for the next century.

With these three major nations muddling along at best, we turn to the four remaining G-7 countries with the most economic clout, a knowledge base, and standards of transparency — the characteristics most necessary to lead in the new knowledge economy.

In spite of Chancellor Kohl's recent defeat, Germany is still mired in its efforts to integrate its two recently reunified parts, the former West Germany and East Germany, into the European Union. Such efforts leave it little desire or energy to restructure the economy and challenge its own powerful labour movement and business community to rise above their own interests. Germany is paying and will continue to pay a very steep price for its emphasis on domestic affairs, understandable though its focus on them may be. The country is beginning to find its ability to compete decisively on the world stage severely compromised even now.

# The Hollowing-Out of Germany

Rather than embrace serious change, many of Germany's mightiest companies are "hollowing out" their operations. This means the companies are following a policy of moving their production outside the country and aggressively expanding and acquiring other companies offshore. Volkswagen has bought SEAT in Spain, Skoda in the Czech Republic, Rolls-Royce in England, and may now be eyeing Volvo in Sweden. Similarly, BMW has bought Rover in England, and Daimler-Benz has acquired Chrysler in the United States.

Volkswagen has already moved one of its product lines to the Skoda works in the Czech Republic, and the new VW Bug is being manufactured in Mexico. Daimler-Benz manufactures its luxury sport-utility vehicles in Alabama, and then exports them back to its home market. It never even considered manufacturing the vehicles in Germany, opting instead to target the North American market and ship back enough units to satisfy the European market and Middle East potentates.

The same hollowing-out trends can be discerned in Germany's publishing industry and in its industrial machinery industry. While the hollowing-out ensures the future of Germany's major corporations through lower costs abroad, which offset the country's onerously high domestic cost-structure, hollowing-out eventually weakens a country's economy. By the year 2000, for example, the huge Siemens corporation will employ more people abroad than it does at home. Siemens has its home appliances and telephone and computer systems manufactured in Brazil and is endeavouring to subcontract as much of its production of components for its gas turbine power generation division to suppliers outside German borders.

As a result, unemployment in Germany has exceeded the unheard-of level of 10 percent. At the same time the country's competitive position slipped internationally to 14th place in the world.

## Now We Are Three

Japan, France, Italy, and Germany having rendered themselves incapable of leading the new world economy, the remaining powers of the G-7 are left to contend for global leadership between themselves — Canada, the United States, and the United Kingdom. The powerful common thread among them? Why, the English language and the capacity of these three countries to harness the powers of the Internet and electronic commerce. Statistics published in the *Computer Industry Almanac* say it all: Together, the G-3 dominate the world's information highway, accounting for

- 43.3 percent of the computers used around the world,
- 47.8 percent of the world's computing power, as measured by millions of instructions per second (MIPS), and
- the lowest international telephone costs in the world.

Unlike other great economic and financial empires in history that have ebbed and waned, dominating a single economic model before withdrawing from centre stage, the United States sets a new standard as the first great power to dominate two different economic models in a row. As the mightiest manufacturing economy of this century, the United States has smoothly assumed a formidable lead in the knowledge economy that follows. The nation is also in the process of converting its past wealth into tremendous growth for the future.

Canada and Britain each have a powerful role to play as the other partners in this economic trinity. Canada has burst onto the international political stage fully in command of the kind of organizational challenges facing the world. As peacekeepers we set an influential example in the creation of international armed forces, operating under the aegis of the United Nations. Our country's drive to establish an International Criminal Court has extended the rule of law beyond national boundaries and self-interest. Finally, at a recent G-7 meeting Canada encouraged the formation of an international regulatory body that would oversee global capital flows.

Across the Atlantic, the United Kingdom spearheads the New Europe. The nation has applied deregulation, privatization, and risk-taking to the social welfare systems and social consensus that underscored the Old Europe, and has been a model for Ireland, the Netherlands, and many others.

## Prognosis for Asia

The globalization we have known is about to be replaced by fragmentation. The G-7 countries are breaking into two camps: one camp is seeking to restructure, deregulate, and privatize its economies, and is led by the United States and Canada in North America and by the United Kingdom in Europe. It stands in stark contrast to the other camp which seeks to preserve social solidarity. This camp is led by Japan in Asia and Germany, France, and Italy in Europe.

Asian economies will have the luxury of choosing sides. The pressure for them to restructure will be lessened and, as Indonesia has done, they will tend to subsitute halfhearted attempts at reform for serious systemic change. Maintaining social cohesion rather than economic strength, as demonstrated by Japan, will appeal to Asia's former tigers; existing hierarchies can be preserved more easily in this camp than in that of the U.S.-led members. Singapore, thus far, stands alone in the U.S. camp and champions privatization, transparency, and restructuring in Asia.

The managing partnership the G-7 established has fractured into two differing visions: One emphasizes growth, technology, private enterprise, transparency, and flexibility. The other stresses the state acting in the national economy, interactive partnering, and an aggressive orientation towards exports. As some countries move faster than others into the knowledge economy, the fault-line between commercial success and social welfare will deepen this tension.

Countries such as Canada demonstrate a long tradition of commercial success *and* social responsibility. They are therefore best equipped to act as global broker and influence leader between these increasingly disparate camps. Canada has a one-time chance to define and create the New Global model. We can play a tremendous part in drafting the next chapter in our civilization.

If Canada fails to heed the call of a new global vision for growth and prosperity in the knowledge economy of the twenty-first century, then it is only a matter of time until some other nation or group of nations leaps at this role. The challenge posed by the up-and-coming economies of Ireland, the Netherlands, Finland, Denmark, Norway, and tiny, aggressive Singapore is too great for Canada to ignore. As Stuart Smally, Al Franken's character on *Saturday Night Live*, might have said, they're smart enough, they're honest enough, and, gosh darn it, people like them. Formidable competition, indeed.

## Up and Coming Economies

| COUNTRY | COMPETITIVENESS RANK | KNOWLEDGE RATIO | CORRUPTION PERCEPTION RANK | AVERAGE 5-YEAR GROWTH |
|---------|---------------------|-----------------|----------------------------|------------------------|
| Singapore | 2 | 37.3 | 9 | 8.5% |
| Netherlands | 4 | 44.1 | 6 | 2.4% |
| Finland | 5 | 33.3 | 2 | 3.5% |
| Norway | 6 | 32.4 | 7 | 3.6% |
| Denmark | 8 | 36.7 | 1 | 2.6% |
| Ireland | 11 | 31.2 | 12 | 7.0% |

Sources: ILO, Institute for Management Development, and
Transparency International

## Big Is Back

As the nations of the world align themselves in one of these two camps, the world's first truly giant or "super-cap" companies will emerge, each wielding enormous stock market capitalizations and presence. Beyond the economic downturn now facing the global economy, this will be one of the more immediate economic consequences of the seismic shifts reshaping the world's economy.

We see the first intimations of these shifts today, in the growing uncertainty and volatility of world markets, including the decline of the Canadian dollar and the emergence of the U.S. dollar as the strongest currency on the planet. Perfect conditions for encouraging large corporations to merge into giant ones, many of whose assets exceed the GDP of some of the nations in which they do business.

The sheer size and market clout of these behemoths will define the progress of a new kind of globalization — corporate vs. political/geographical. For example, the intended mergers of Canadian banks — Royal Bank with Bank of Montreal, and CIBC with TD — are natural, even inevitable, outcomes of the decline of the G-7. Internationally, AT&T's partnership with British Telecom, to cite another example, signifies the preliminary stirring of these giants who will eventually roam the planet, intent on marking out their individual territories.

Enormous turf wars will break out between them, punctuated by aggressive market expansions and complete transformations of their target markets. The participants will be motivated more and more to capture larger and larger shares of the rising incomes of an estimated 45 million knowledge workers — in North America alone. But do these massive changes illustrate mere corporate greed, or in fact corporate fear driving the emergence of this brave new world of corporate giants?

The small-business era we have witnessed in North America is also coming to an end. In its place, the philosophy of "big is back" is settling in, thanks to deepening corporate fears that the knowledge economy threatens the very foundations of big business's hold on economic power.

Knowledge workers and savvy Internet users everywhere are a force destroying the established profit margins of the big corporations. Through electronic commerce, these workers are pushing down banking service fees, pressing for reduced management expense ratios in mutual funds, deep-discounting on airline fares and wiping out the traditional profit margins on books (Have you *seen* those discounts at Amazon.com?). This collective flexing of this group's muscles marks the early stirrings of a rising consumer power that traditional business interests consider deeply menacing.

But remember that every new economy also gives birth to completely new companies that eventually outgrow their predecessors, thus putting the lie to the old truism that there is nothing new under the sun. As clear-cut as some of these battles may appear to us on the surface at this point, we cannot begin to predict the full extent of the changes the New Economy has in store for us.

# THE WEALTH OF INDUSTRIES AND NATIONS

We in the 1990s may not be accustomed to thinking of specific industries or companies as wielding more power than entire nations do. Throughout history the balance of economic power between commercial enterprise and the state has ebbed and flowed, back and forth. Yet, in some ways, there is nothing fundamentally new about all these changes facing us now.

As far back as the city-states of ancient Greece, wealthy merchant families dominated certain lines of commerce. The Medici family of the fifteenth century ruled much of Italy before the political pendulum swung back, and the unification of Italy tolled the end of such individual families' local monopolies. The Rothschild family of the nineteenth century, the great corporate dynasties of the Astors, the Rockefellers, and the Morgans oversaw industries larger than most of the world's economies in their days. Bill Gates's personal fortune of US$50 billion today exceeds the gross domestic product of 131 countries.

This tension, while not recognized officially for what it is — or for being a potentially constructive force — can sometimes turn utterly destructive, turning into a contest between the rule of commerce and that of the will of high-placed kings or dictators and the will of the people. History traces such conflicts through epic wars, conquests of wealth, acts of treachery, and various alliances. Fortunately for me and my consulting firm, we can also measure this balance and its shifts as they happen in our economy today.

In a very enlightening study my firm conducted that monitored the various sizes and growth of 476 North American industries and compared them with the economies of 40 different nations, three important trends became evident. Each gave me pause.

First — and it cannot be repeated too often — the balance of international economic power has swung swiftly and decisively to favour North America. Internationally, the return-to-risk

prefers investment and corporate strategies that emphasize industries over countries, and large companies over small.

Canadian companies and industries must redefine their strategies for growth and focus their energies on the U.S. market, home
to many of the world's largest and fastest growing industries.

Second, for governments in Canada, the challenge will be to
redefine themselves in terms of the knowledge economy's new
demands. This will mean finding balances between the behemoth
industries and companies that are coming of age in this New
Economy and the enormous power of the knowledge worker in
reshaping entire markets and industries.

Our governments — federal, provincial and territorial, and
municipal — have concentrated on meeting the needs of the
small-business sector since the early 1980s. We hear about the
big handouts to the Bombardiers of the world, the millions in
loans that haven't been repaid to fund R & D and growth. Meanwhile, governments at all levels involve themselves in the
deHavilland–Boeing deals. These are hardly small companies.
But scattered examples aside, there is no mistaking the major
thrust of government support in the small business sector of this
country through a variety of programs from the Business Development Bank, IRAP (the National Research Council's Industrial
Research Assistance Program) and the Export Development
Corporation, to name just three. As this era draws to a close,
governments must grapple with the needs, wants, wishes, and
demands of whole industries and companies that are larger and
more powerful economically than the governments themselves
are or could ever become.

Third, we consumers — and increasingly knowledge workers
— must define our own role as the strategic assets and proprietors
of the knowledge driving this economy into and through the
twenty-first century. The question we have to answer is this:
*Whose* knowledge-based economy will it be, anyway? In other

145

words, what groups, new "interests," or sectors will control it? Will it be the knowledge workers who, after all, are the owners of such knowledge, or will it be the companies who employ them?

## The Emergence of the New Globalization

What lies beneath the surface facts and figures, then, is the remarkable story of one continent's metamorphosis from old to new, and the maturing of Canada's even more remarkable capacity to script a whole new chapter in human development. The wealth and breadth of our nation's accomplishments are laying the groundwork for a New Economy beyond what we can imagine right now. It's the story of the century and it's going to make your pulse race.

# 6

# THE GREAT AGE OF
# FINANCIAL SURPLUSES

In the first three months of 1998, the mighty U.S. economy generated US$57.8 billion *more* in national wealth than it had an immediate use for, that's at the rate of a cool US$19 billion a month! And that's not all. For all of 1997, the American economy generated a financial surplus of US$215.5 billion and in the 1990s, it has amassed a staggering US$1.3 *trillion* more in national capital than it had an immediate use for.

*Welcome to the world of financial surpluses!*

To put these colossal surpluses into perspective, the United States economy raked in enough cash in the 1990s to *buy* Africa — the entire continent — outright. If Russia put itself on the auction block (not a bad idea, given the economic mess it's in!), and were to value its economy on its national output or GDP (Gross Domestic Product) of US$460 billion, then the United States could *purchase* Russia and have hundreds of billions in change left over.

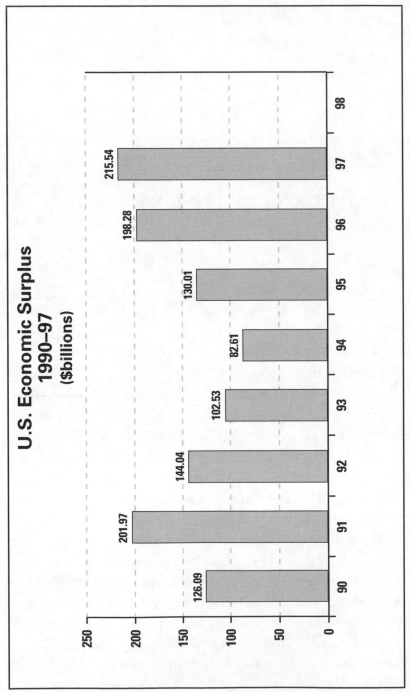

U.S. Economic Surplus
1990–97
($billions)

| Year | Value |
|------|-------|
| 90 | 126.09 |
| 91 | 201.97 |
| 92 | 144.04 |
| 93 | 102.53 |
| 94 | 82.61 |
| 95 | 130.01 |
| 96 | 198.28 |
| 97 | 215.54 |

Sources: U.S. Department of Commerce, Nuala Beck & Associates Inc.

Looked at from another perspective, America's financial surpluses in the 1990s dwarf the country's entire creation of surpluses or financial wealth from the 1950s to the 1970s *inclusive*. See the chart below.

Is it any wonder that U.S. interest rates are at such low levels? Or that the U.S. stock market, as measured by the Dow, has risen a stunning 225 percent in the 1990s? Hence the U.S. dollar is becoming the strongest currency on the planet and price inflation is a thing of the past in an economy that is creating so much wealth that the federal government no longer needs to print money or indulge in monetary excesses.

## U.S. Economic Surplus
## 1952–98 (Year to Date)
### ($billions)

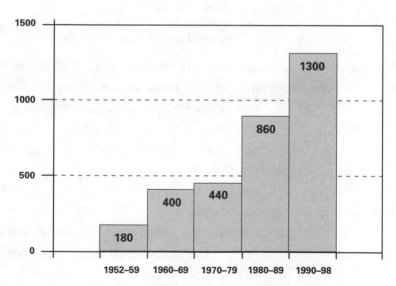

Sources: U.S. Department of Commerce, Nuala Beck & Associates Inc.

## Canada's Economic Deficit
## 1962–98 (Year to Date)
### ($billions)

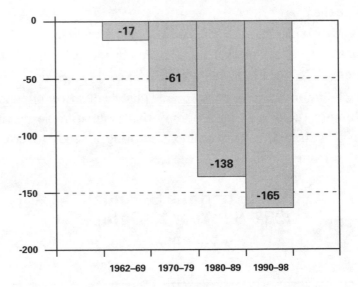

Sources: Statistics Canada, Nuala Beck & Associates Inc.

If you're not quite sure what a financial surplus is, you're not alone. We Canadians have become accustomed to living a life of deficits in a country that has never had enough capital to go around. Except when it comes to selling resources, the concept of a surplus is utterly foreign to us. Since the building and expansion of the great railroads, Canada has been a nation of systemic deficit producers and has had to beg or borrow the money needed to finance its growth and its needs.

Now the time has come for all Canadians to learn what a financial surplus is because, believe it or not, Canada is also on its way to becoming a nation with money to burn.

# A New Financial World

Divide up Canada's economy, or any country's economy, into its five major components, and you will readily understand where deficits and surpluses come from.

1. First, there are the individual consumers, you and me. We either live within our means and have a little left over, or we face personal bankruptcy by allowing our personal deficits to get out of hand. For every 1,000 Canadians 2.7 opted to or were forced into declaring bankruptcy in the 1990s, double the bankruptcy rate of the 1980s: slumping house prices in many parts of Canada, sky-high credit-card debt, small businesses that failed to cover their costs — all played a part in the erosion of Canada's personal sector surplus.

2. Then, there's the federal government. Either it lives within its means or it doesn't. Tax revenues can cover the government's spending and interest costs or they fall short, in which case the government generates a deficit. By the year end of 1997, the federal government had a surplus of CDN$6.2 billion, the first such annual surplus in over 20 years.

3. Provincial governments must also choose whether to keep their spending in line with their revenues or go into debt. By the year end of 1997, the provinces had a financial surplus of CDN$1.3 billion, a welcome change from the string of financial deficits since 1990.

4. Crown corporations used to be notorious deficit producers and operated almost as a matter of course below the zero line. Their era of systemic deficits has given way to greater fiscal responsibility for two reasons. First, because some of the largest crown corporations, like Air Canada and CN, have been privatized, which has simply meant the end of deficits. Privatizing companies like Air Canada hasn't caused

planes to fall out of the sky, nor has it led to soaring airfares, as some among the most ideologically entrenched supporters of government ownership had predicted. The second reason why crown corps are producing only tiny deficits of $1.2 billion in 1997 is that they, along with the rest of us, have had to tighten their belts by working harder and smarter.

5. Next comes corporate Canada, a mixed lot. In 1997, it plunged back into deficit, this time to the tune of CDN$14.5 billion. Its members should be ashamed of themselves. Corporate cash flows fell short of the funds required for capital spending, inventories, and a frenzy of costly takeovers. Individual companies should not have bought companies they couldn't afford.

Add the above surpluses and subtract the deficits and you have calculated Canada's financial and economic standing, as shown in the chart on the following page.

# Living on Other People's Money

The irony is unmistakable. After years of hearing Canadian business leaders preach that government must learn to live within its means and citing government deficits as the root of all evils, the shoe is now on the other foot! Companies don't hesitate to commit themselves to mergers and aquisitions they can't afford. Nor do many bosses hesitate at the thought of spending millions and billions of our national savings on new facilities. While you or I might make do with a kitchen renovation or a secondhand vehicle in the driveway, many companies have made a mockery of their own lean-and-mean slogans by spending borrowed funds with corporate largesse. Corporate Canada now makes government look lean, restrained, and fiscally responsible!

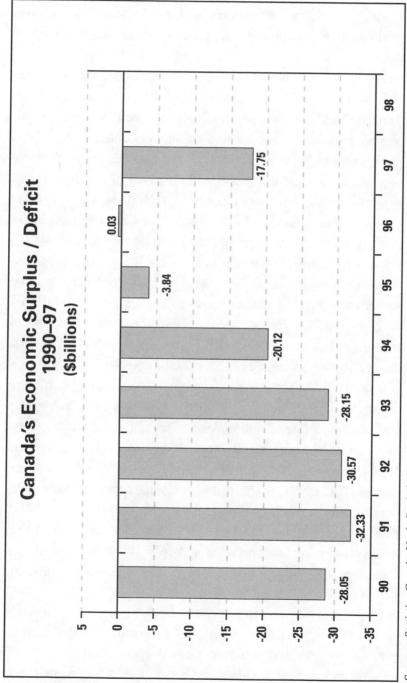

Canada's Economic Surplus / Deficit
1990–97
($billions)

Sources: Statistics Canada, Nuala Beck & Associates Inc.

153

Meanwhile, senior executives wonder why today's knowledge workers have little or no respect for the companies that employ them. (See Chapter 7.)

The first complaint that I am going to hear from corporate strategists within whining distance of Bay Street, as they read my demand that Corporate Canada eliminate its deficit, is that companies are *supposed* to borrow and use other people's money. I can just hear the old guard in finance departments demanding to know how in God's name the widows and orphans of this country are expected to survive if they cannot invest their savings in companies that pay them interest and dividends? And what about the entire banking system? And what of the important role the banks have played for centuries as intermediaries bringing together lenders and borrowers into one peaceful and happy financial system? Surely the *new* economics of the late twentieth century must be a plot to destabilize the old and righteous boards of directors who have approved corporate Canada's financial deficits so eagerly, which in the first quarter of 1998 amounted to CDN$2.6 billion.

Too many CEOs have lost sight of the fact that they're supposed to create wealth, not deficits. One look at our neighbour corporate America should make this crystal clear: while corporate Canada accumulated $50 billion in financial deficits in the 1990s, corporate America generated financial surpluses to the tune of US$21 billion. This difference underlies the equally striking disparity in stock market performance: Canada's TSE 300 is 87.1 percent higher, but the U.S. S&P 500 has risen 240.2 percent between January 1990 and July 1998. No wonder the Canadian dollarette has been battered when measured against the U.S. dollar.

The contrasting charts on pages 149 and 150 show America's steady march, year by year, into megasurpluses, and Canada's equally steady march into deeper and deeper deficits.

Now, before you decide that Canada is heading to hell in a

handcart, consider two important facts: first, that although the Canadian dollar is weak against the U.S. dollar, it has displayed formidable strength against the German Mark, French Franc and countless other currencies in the first half of 1998.

Second, Canada's lingering deficit problem is no longer the result of government spending. Our governments are now moving sure-footedly into surpluses that will allow them to cut taxes, which in turn will allow us taxpayers to save or spend as we see fit. The remaining national deficit in our country is a left-over from the old industries slow to shake off their lingering addictions to debt. That too is in the process of changing today. Why? Building an old economy was frightfully expensive, but building a New Economy isn't, as technology prices continuously plummet. It's just another fact of life in a New Economy.

# The 77.5 Percent Solution

I remember the intense fascination within Nuala Beck & Associates Inc. a couple of years ago when my colleagues confirmed that 35.7 percent of the TSE 300 was now firmly rooted in the New Economy. Here was the hard evidence that the new technology-driven economy had spread well beyond tiny start-up companies and now had an impressive presence on the TSE 300. The speed and size of this shift assured me that Canada was not the hopeless cause that some in the early 1990s believed it to be as old industries downsized and as recession deepened.

Canada's stock market was being given a new lease on life thanks to the wealth-creating capabilities of new and dynamic industries. These represented our future. Equally clear was the fact that the United States was further ahead than Canada. That was to be expected, as the United States was, after all, the birthplace of the New Economy.

THE NEXT
CENTURY
WHY
CANADA
WINS

Now, only five years after that first exciting discovery, a colossal 77.5 percent of the TSE 300's market value is firmly planted in the fertile wealth creating ground of the New Economy. And Canada's knowledge base has surpassed that of the United States.

The effect of this shift in Canada from old wealth-consuming industries to the new wealth-creating ones shows up vividly in the stock market: between 1995 and July 1998 the New Economy Index measuring the performance of that 77.5 percent of the TSE 300 outperformed the overall TSE 300 by a very wide margin.

## Performance, Performance, Performance

*Annual compound returns for 1, 3, 5 and 10 years to July 1998*

|         | NEW ECONOMY | TSE 300 | OLD ECONOMY | WATCH LIST |
|---------|-------------|---------|-------------|------------|
| 1-year  | 16.5        | 2.4     | -14.8       | -24.1      |
| 3-year  | 27.0        | 16.7    | 4.9         | 6.4        |
| 5-year  | 20.6        | 14.2    | 11.1        | 5.8        |
| 10-year | 13.4        | 10.5    | 8.9         | 8.6        |

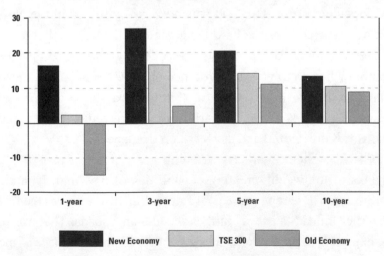

## Total Annual Compound Returns (%) July 1998

Sources: Toronto Stock Exchange, Nuala Beck & Associates Inc.

If Canada's old economy companies, the ones generating all the deficits, can turn themselves into wealth creators, then you can be sure of the fact that the Canadian dollar will stabilize — and even recover some of the ground it has lost recently.

# THE MONEY CYCLE

At a time when such new realities skew traditional economic theory by mocking the once-predictable relationship between excess capacity, growth, inflation, and unemployment, two lesser known hypotheses are worthy of careful attention. Together, they foretell the end of Canadian deficits and the emergence of Canada as a powerhouse nation.

The Life Cycle hypothesis has little to do with working those extra pounds off at the gym. Simply but brilliantly the hypothesis explains that as we go through life we as individuals enter fairly predictable stages of earning, borrowing, and saving for retirement. The trick is to figure out which stage we're in. Then the long-term direction of interest rates and the stock market becomes easier to predict.

According to the Life Cycle hypothesis, in our first jobs we usually see our incomes rise as we gain valuable experience and become increasingly productive. In mid life, our earnings potential usually flattens out as we reach the peak of our earnings power. After this point we see our income drop either a little or a lot, depending on how well we saved for our retirement years.

But throughout our lives another hypothesis quietly applies to our working lives. The Permanent Income hypothesis demonstrates that people strive to maintain a fairly steady standard of living over the course of their lives. Short on this income, young people will borrow to finance that first stereo and bedroom set, and it's not unusual for them to take a large mortgage on a first

**157**

home or condo, secure in the knowledge that a lifetime of earn-ing power will lessen the burden of their monthly payments. Later on in life, empty nesters usually live below the lifestyle they could now afford, often choosing instead to save the extra disposable income in their RRSPs or in lump sum payments to pay off the mortgage, or both. Thus the early years of borrowing are deftly replaced by the latter years of savings, people all the while seeking to preserve some sense of permanence or predictability in their lifestyles.

Now, all of this would remain relevant to individuals only, if it were not for the fact that the largest proportion of our population are moving en masse through each stage.

Baby boomers, savvy about demographics, understand instinctively their enormous influence on money and markets through their sheer numbers. As a group, they know that their influence on the economy has been enormous. That is why the impact of these two hypotheses together is important.

Three stages make up this money cycle. I'm now going to describe what happens to inflation, interest rates, government spending, the stock market, wealth management, and many other facets of our economic future when a whole hoard of baby boomers moves simultaneously along the curve I have drawn for you on page 159. You can easily picture where you or your family fit depending on what stage you are at in your own life cycle.

# Life Cycle Hypothesis and Permanent Income Hypothesis

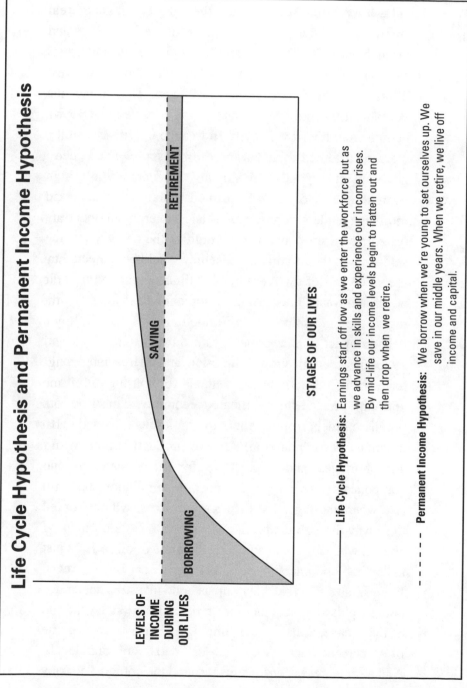

**LEVELS OF INCOME DURING OUR LIVES**

BORROWING

SAVING

RETIREMENT

**STAGES OF OUR LIVES**

——— **Life Cycle Hypothesis:** Earnings start off low as we enter the workforce but as we advance in skills and experience our income rises. By mid-life our income levels begin to flatten out and then drop when we retire.

– – – – – **Permanent Income Hypothesis:** We borrow when we're young to set ourselves up. We save in our middle years. When we retire, we live off income and capital.

Source: Nuala Beck & Associates Inc.

1.  **The Borrowing Years.** When the baby boom generation entered the labour market en masse in the late 1960s and through the 1970s, they needed jobs, housing, furniture, and cars, and fast. They wanted to maintain the standard of living that their parents had achieved. Remember the Permanent Income hypothesis? It was expected that young people would borrow heavily to finance the lifestyles they were accustomed to and wanted to preserve. The Federal government responded by shifting the economy into high gear: the Bank of Canada printed money for banks and mortgage lenders to pass along. Big government-spending programs ensured that as the youth of the country left the safety net of their family homes, they would be protected by the safety net of a government willing to respond to their needs and wants, thus easing — some might say, just delaying — their transition into adulthood.

The impact of the *money cycle* through the 1960s and 1970s on economic growth, inflation, and interest rates could have been predicted: the big demand for housing, furniture, and cars created an overheated economy. This flood of purchase orders from retailers to wholesalers, passed on to manufacturers, created all sorts of production bottlenecks and shortages, and price hikes for many materials and components. As you would expect, price inflation started to rise when shortages led to price increases, which worked their way through the production process. It didn't help, of course, when OPEC quadrupled the price of oil in 1972 just as the baby boomers were in their prime car-buying years. Interest rates eventually shot up as bond investors demanded better yields to protect them from rising inflation. By the end of the decade, inflation was running at a year-over-year rate of 9.8 percent. Interest rates had soared to double digit levels. And a brutal recession was just around the corner. The baby boom generation needed only so many houses or cars or stereos before moving on to satisfy other needs and wants.

2. **The Transition of the 1980s.** The shift away from an economy driven by demand for housing and big-ticket consumer durables wreaked havoc in the world of manufacturing in the 1980s. Prices couldn't be raised in softening markets, interest rates on the debt many companies had incurred to expand plants and buy equipment in the 1970s became crippling as orders fell below the levels planned for. Thus companies began eyeing export markets for their products. Free trade between Canada and the United States moved into newspaper front pages.

On their way and launched into jobs and homes of their own, baby boomers sat back to enjoy their lifestyles through the 1980s. By this point cappucino makers and food processing gizmos were necessities that you didn't need to take out a mortgage or bank loan to buy. You simply used a credit card. Mortgages were paid down, and the roaring inflation of the 1970s cooled. Meanwhile, maxing out the household credit cards became the sport of the moment for this powerful segment of the population. Although interest rates on credit card balances stayed high, interest rates in general peaked in 1981 with bank prime rates falling from 22.8 percent to 13.5 percent by the end of the 1980s. Pressure mounted for governments to rein in their own deficits, which they initially did with little enthusiasm. Old habits die hard.

However, the magnitude of this shift from spending and borrowing to saving and investment, however halting it might sometimes have appeared, marked a sea change in the very underpinnings of consumer activity. A nation of die-hard borrowers metamorphosed into a nation of die-hard savers as we marched predictably along the Life Cycle curve.

**161**

3. **The Saving and Investing Years.** The 1990s mark the beginning of a twenty-five-year period of intense savings and investment as Canadian baby boomers invest mightily for their retirement years in the next century. As Professor David Foot, Canada's leading authority on demographics and author of *Boom, Bust & Echo*, has so aptly pointed out, the years ahead will prove a bonanza to the mutual fund business in Canada. Why? Because the majority of Canadians will be living below their income levels and saving the difference. As a result we will see continued long-term upward pressure on stock prices and further declines in interest rates. It's only a matter of time until free money becomes a North American norm.

# Free Money

Pick up a weekend newspaper, flip to the automotive section, and you'll see an example of free money staring you in the face: 0 percent financing rates! If you have an interest in home furnishings or in, say, a new washer-dryer, you won't have far to look for free money for at least the first six months, and often longer. It's not unusual to see home builders offering free money, too, zero interest on a home mortgage for a specified period.

Rapidly growing technology companies already understand free money. Many raise capital by issuing shares on the market. Their rapid growth assures shareholders already investing in these companies that dilution will be negligible. Many companies have raised hundreds of millions of dollars, acquiring the money literally free of charge.

The important link between the great era of financial surpluses and interest rates is shown with stunning clarity in the chart on page 164. As America, the New Economy trendsetter, enjoys rising financial surpluses, U.S. interest rates decline. Once these rates fall to the level at which service charges exceed deposit rates, a new breed of finance will have been born in North America, ushering in the era of free money.

In 1981, when home mortgages hit a peak of 22 percent and Canada's inflation rate hovered at 13 percent, it was unimaginable that mortgage rates could ever fall to the current 7 percent, their lowest levels in over 30 years. It was equally inconceivable to the baby boom generation that by the time they reached the middle years of their lives money would become available for free to well-managed households.

As a newlywed in the 1970s I heard over and over the stories from my in-laws and well-meaning aunts and uncles of the days when mortgages could be had for as little as 6 ¼! Like most of my generation, I didn't need a math degree to figure out that two incomes were a flat-out necessity until mortgage rates dropped below 12 ½ percent (think of those bygone days as a time that required his and hers mortgages of 6 ¼ percent *each*). But all of that has changed profoundly with mortgage interest rates that have ratcheted back down to the levels where a single paycheque can support a house and car and reasonably good lifestyle. Don't be surprised if the next century sees the return to the single paycheque for a family, or households in which both partners opt for part-time work. It won't require much more than two half paycheques (or one full one) to live a comfortable life in the decades ahead of us. If you invest money in mutual funds or plan to build a retirement nest egg in the years ahead, this era of free money will pave the way for some of the most exciting stock market gains in history. And it is conceivable that baby boomers will retire on pensions far more generous than they have come to expect, even in their wildest dreams.

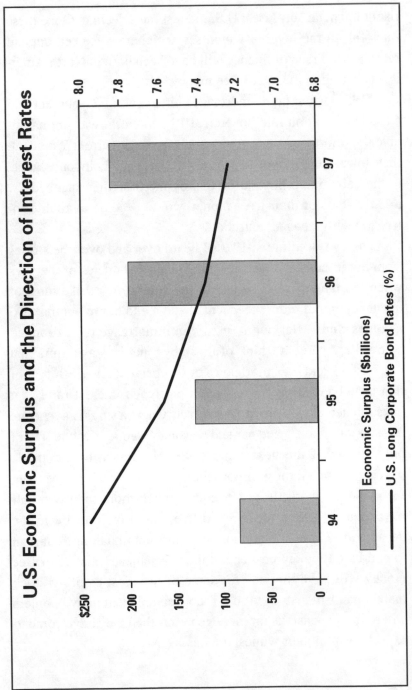

## U.S. Economic Surplus and the Direction of Interest Rates

Economic Surplus ($billions)

U.S. Long Corporate Bond Rates (%)

Source: U.S. Department of Commerce

164

# The Ancient Art of Modern Portfolio Management

Talk to any financial adviser and she or he will tell you that stock market portfolios can be managed according to one of three very different styles.

- The *value manager* seeks to buy shares in undervalued companies with a view to holding them for the longer term. This manager believes the stock market will recognize the hidden value eventually and drive the share price higher.
- The *growth manager* seeks out companies on the fast track and is more concerned with the future of the company than with whether the stock is presently undervalued.
- The *sector-rotator manager,* meanwhile, focuses more on whether the industry is hot. This manager will move in and out of industries depending on what stage of the business cycle he or she believes is closest at hand.

If you find all of this confusing, take comfort from the fact that portfolio managers themselves are just as confused about the principles that underpin investment management in this knowledge-based economy.

What each of these groups of portfolio managers have failed to realize to date is that the investment tools that they rely on are no longer reliable gauges of value, growth, or the business cycle. Essentially paid the big bucks to outperform the stock market, these managers are discovering they cannot do so anymore.

Of Canada's 298 equity funds in existence as of July 1998, only 15 outperformed our New Economy Index (the 77.5 percent of the TSE 300 that is in the New Economy) on a one-year basis, and only 2 managed to outperform our New Economy Index on a five-year basis. (The table on the following page shows the

**165**

actual performance of the index and the mere handful of Canadian equity funds that beat this new performance benchmark.)

But before jumping to conclusions, we should ask why so many of the best and brightest portfolio managers in the country are having such obvious difficulty outperforming our New Economy Index during the most spectacular bull market in the last half century. A little history will help explain why many of the smartest money managers in the country just aren't measuring up.

## New Economy Performance

| AS AT JULY 31, 1998 | 1-YEAR GROWTH | 5-YEAR GROWTH |
|---|---|---|
| New Economy Index | 16.5% | 20.6% |
| AIC Advantage | | 33.0% |
| FGF Equity (04/97) | | 23.9% |
| Rothschild Canadian Equity (09/97) | 32.2% | |
| Universal Canadian Growth (04/98) | 29.2% | |
| Quebec Growth Fund | 28.6% | |
| Universal Canadian Growth US$ (04/98) | 26.2% | |
| AIC Diversified Canada | 21.8% | |
| Pursuit Growth (05/98) | 21.7% | |
| AIC Advantage II | 21.4% | |
| Pursuit Growth US$ | 21.0% | |
| Standard Life Ideal Equity (12/97) | 19.5% | |
| Associate Investor Ltd. | 19.3% | |
| CB Canadian (05/98) | 18.0% | |
| Infinity Canadian | 17.5% | |
| Cundill Security A | 17.2% | |
| Cundill Security B | 16.8% | |
| Empire Group Equity (02/98) | 16.8% | |

Sources: Nuala Beck & Associates Inc., www.Fundlibrary.com

# A [VERY] BRIEF HISTORY OF INVESTMENT MANAGEMENT

When Benjamin Graham and David Dodd published their seminal work on security analysis in 1934, they invented what became the profession of financial analysis for the purpose of investing. They introduced the radical new concept of "value" investing and showed how investors could avoid speculating by rigorously analyzing a company's financial statements. This way they could determine whether its shares were under- or overvalued in the stock market. They counselled investors to seek out companies that represented good longer term value, through applying financial ratios, among them P/Es (which measure the earnings of a company against the price of its stock). With this information an investor could determine how far into the future the stock market had already discounted the company's earnings.

But with the U.S. S&P index recently trading at a P/E of 26 and the TSE 300 trading at 30 times earnings in mid 1998, Ben Graham and Dave Dodd would undoubtedly roll over in their graves. They would think investors had lost their wits, paying such lofty prices for investment-grade stocks.

These investment pioneers would be equally puzzled by the growth in earnings, which for the technology-laden Nasdaq index has soared 327 percent in the last decade. TSE 300 Index earnings over the same period have risen almost 100 percent, outstripping the earnings growth in any earlier decade this century. Growth managers too often find themselves adrift, unable to adequately gauge the very growth they seek to capture. Old methods of estimating a company's earnings potential yield little useful information when so much of its earnings are based on such intangibles as its knowledge base.

What about the business cycle? Sector rotators find themselves at just as much a loss because the business cycle itself has changed profoundly. Why, Graham and Dodd wouldn't even recognize it

**167**

today. So many of the industries — from airlines to computers—
didn't even exist in the 1930s. Similarly, inventories no longer play
the part they once did in our just-in-time-production world. New
Economy companies frequently carry little debt and are therefore
less exposed to the impact of interest rates. Recessions have short-
ened remarkably in their duration from an average of eighteen
months in Graham and Dodd's time to the micro-recessions of
today's technology-driven product cycles.

## Average Duration of Recessions in the United States

| NUMBER OF BUSINESS CYCLES | DATE | AVERAGE DURATION OF RECESSIONS | AVERAGE DURATION OF RECOVERIES |
|---|---|---|---|
| 34 | 1834 to 1982 | 19 months | 32 months |
| 5 | 1834 to 1855 | 24 months | 26 months |
| 16 | 1854 to 1945 | 22 months | 27 months |
| 6 | 1919 to 1945 | 18 months | 35 months |
| 8 | 1945 to 1982 | 11 months | 45 months |
| 3 | 1983 to 1997 | 10 months | 21 months |

Sources: Nuala Beck & Associates Inc., U.S. Department of Commerce

The table below illustrates the New Economy and the length of
time that micro-recessions lasted.

## Duration of Micro-Recessions

| FROM | TO | DURATION |
|---|---|---|
| May 1985 | Nov 1985 | 7 months |
| Jan 1986 | May 1986 | 5 months |
| Nov 1986 | Nov 1986 | 1 Month |
| March 1989 | July 1989 | 5 months |
| May 1991 | Nov 1991 | 7 months |

Source: Nuala Beck & Associates Inc.

Today's micro-recession lasts less than six months. By the time economists receive the data on one, the recession has almost ended!

You can see the new business cycle for yourself and how it's changing in the chart on the next page.

The impact of this knowledge economy and its micro-recessions is especially pronounced in North America's financial world. Here stock markets have defied the forecasts of even the most brazen optimists. Since 1990 the TSE 300's performance has exceeded the performance of the Canadian market over the last 50 years! From the start of the great bull market in October 1990 to the middle of 1998, Canada's TSE 300 generated a total return of 125 percent. The Dow Jones Industrial Average at the same time soared 467 percent.

The knowledge economy has changed the fundamentals of investing for the twenty-first century. Graham and Dodd understood, as few others did, that the manufacturing economy of the early twentieth century was changing everything in its path, including the fundamentals of portfolio management.

# Sharks Replacing Bears: The New Norm

Some portfolio managers wait for the world to revert to what it used to be, and wait anxiously for the big bear to lumber out of the giant forest and maul their portfolios to death. Some of Canada's best and brightest investment managers, on the other hand, understand intuitively that there isn't a single industry in this New Economy that lumbers.

The rapid flow of information between companies and their investors globally, and the equally rapid flow of information within a company alerting managers to problems as they emerge, have created structural, systemic changes in stock market behaviour.

**169**

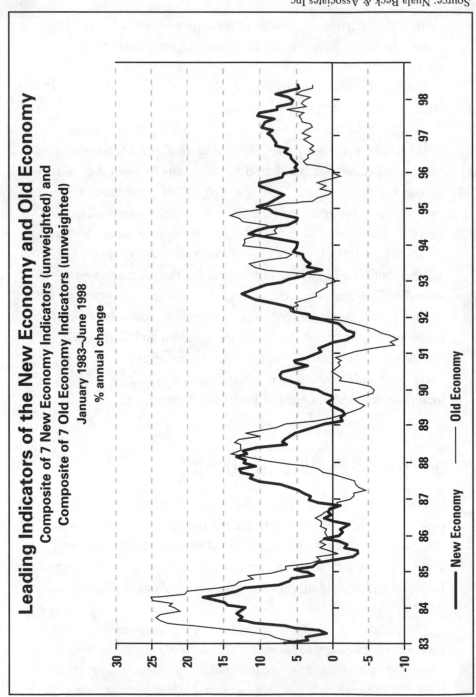

**Leading Indicators of the New Economy and Old Economy**
Composite of 7 New Economy Indicators (unweighted) and
Composite of 7 Old Economy Indicators (unweighted)
January 1983–June 1998
% annual change

New Economy ——— Old Economy ———

Now we are witnessing the emergence of shark attacks rather than the traditional bear markets. Sharks hit fast and viciously, and you're lucky if you escape them with all your limbs intact. The blessing is that they don't last long. Blink and they're over with.

My consulting firm has tracked these new-style shark attacks on a consistent basis. I have summarized the results for you in the following table.

## Shark Attacks versus Bear Markets

| S&P 500 PEAK | TROUGH | DURATION OF DECLINE | MAGNITUDE OF DECLINE |
|---|---|---|---|
| Jan 1973 | Dec 1974 | 23 months | -43.4% Bear Market |
| Sept 1976 | March 1978 | 18 months | -15.7% Correction |
| Nov 1980 | July 1982 | 20 months | -19.4% Bear Market |
| Oct 1983 | July 1984 | 9 months | -9.9% Correction |
| Aug 1987 | Dec 1987 | 4 months | -26.8% 1987 Crash |
| June 1990 | Oct 1990 | 4 months | -14.8% Shark Attack |
| Jan 1992 | March 1992 | 2 months | -2.1% Shark Attack |
| March 1993 | April 1993 | 1 month | -1.6% Shark Attack |
| Jan 1994 | April 1994 | 3 months | -5.4% Shark Attack |
| Sept 1994 | Dec 1994 | 3 months | -2.5% Shark Attack |
| June 1996 | July 1996 | 1 month | -3.7% Shark Attack |
| Feb 1997 | April 1997 | 2 months | -4.3% Shark Attack |
| Sept 1997 | Oct 27, 1997 | 1 month | -6.4% Shark Attack |
| July 1998 | Sept 1998 | 2 months | -12.1% Shark Attack |

Source: Nuala Beck & Associates Inc.

Particularly relevant about this table is the fact that it signals a profound change in the pace and rhythm of stock market performance in North America. A century of *buy and sell* is being replaced by the new philosophy of *buy and hold* as we enter the twenty-first century — a new age of financial surpluses that is overturning everything we once knew about the way money moves and grows.

# 7

# KNOWLEDGE MANAGEMENT

As I've described them in Chapter 1, knowledge workers are a new breed. They live and work by new rules, rules that extend far beyond flex-hours or the right to wear T-shirts to work on Fridays. They are becoming a major force, will be *the* major driving force in twenty-first century labour markets. And all along the way, they're changing how organizations manage, do business, market, and grow.

## ORIGIN OF THE SPECIES

Knowledge workers account for one of every three employees in America. By the summer of 1998 they numbered more than 42 million strong and their ranks continue to swell. Despite a slightly softer job market in 1998, knowledge employment has increased with overall economic growth to the tune of 3.5 percent. This is more than three times higher than the U.S. economy's employment growth rate of 1.1 percent in July 1998.

America's corporate elite of high-knowledge industries depends on their knowledge workers as heavily as General Motors has depended historically on its production workers to keep its assembly lines moving. You can see in the charts on the next page that, while the ranks of production workers continue to dwindle as old industries shrink or gravitate to labour-saving technology, the ranks of knowledge workers in America continue to expand.

High-knowledge industries account for 30.9 percent of Canada's economic output. They also employ four million people, or one in every three Canadians. The four engines driving Canada's New Economy employ a workforce of 1.5 million alone — in the United States, the comparable figure soars to 24.2 million.

The North American workplace is changing on a scale not seen in decades. From a "buyer's market" in the early 1990s, when unemployment rates in Canada and the United States topped the 11 percent and 7 percent mark, respectively — a time when companies could pick and choose from dozens of eager (read "desperate") applicants, the labour market is changing rapidly into a "seller's market." Companies find themselves vying for the attention of prospective employees; once they have hired them, the same companies then face the challenge of keeping them.

Turnover rates among hotel employees now approach 100 percent annually. Yet sharply rising turnover rates are no longer the preserve of low-knowledge, low-wage industries. Industry averages are moving up and, according to the Washington D.C.–based Bureau of National Affairs, the rising rate of employees' leaving jobs (excluding temporary staff's departures and layoffs) has affected all industries. Industry averages across the super-smart, information-technology (IT) services industry range from 25 percent to 30 percent a year. In the back rooms of the financial services industry, for example, employee retention has plummeted as turnover rates approach 40 percent.

# Employment of U.S. Production Workers
## (millions of workers)

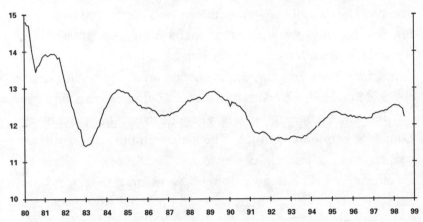

Source: U.S. Bureau of Labor Statistics

# Employment of U.S. Knowledge Workers
## (millions of workers)

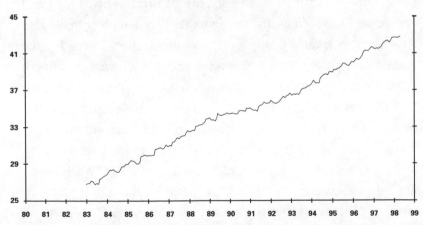

Sources: U.S. Bureau of Labor Statistics, Nuala Beck & Associates Inc.

174

These statistics are interesting in their own right. They signal a profound shift from the fear of job loss palpable in the workplace of the 1990s to a growing employee confidence that companies will do what it takes to keep workers happy — or else some other company will, gladly.

Strong growth in North America will absorb the pool of knowledge workers, so we must prepare for a whole new era of retention strategies, employee benefits, and human resource strategies. Knowledge workers are in the driver's seat, and they know it!

Salary surveys of IT managers and staff, from DataMasters, tell the story: Between 1990 and 1998, Chief Information Officers in the United States saw their median salaries rise 49 percent, while their staff matched them point for point with median increases of the same percentage. In Canada, the software industry enjoyed average salary gains of 7 percent last year alone, well ahead of the 2.1 percent increase for Canada's workforce as a whole.

As labour markets tighten (Canada's unemployment rate has dropped to 8.4 percent and to 4.5 percent in the United States), salaries will rise. The pressure on employers, however, will not be limited to the size of the paycheques they offer — employees will demand new measures to attract and retain these valuable employees. Why?

Because employee turnover rates above 10 percent are too costly for companies and organizations to contemplate for any length of time. The next frontier of cost management is about to switch abruptly.

# New Perks versus Old Perks

The old social contract of job security in exchange for worker loyalty has disappeared, all but destroyed by the downsizings of the 1990s. A new social contract is in the process of emerging.

**175**

Old perks such as the corner office, an expense account, and a company car are rapidly being replaced by new perks: the fastest laptop, cool projects in a neat space, the learning budget.

The hottest retention strategy? It's starting your own Corporate University. Here employees, in addition to acquiring cutting-edge skills, bond and build lifelong friendships and working relationships with their co-workers.

1. **Corporate "U"**: These private fraternities and the teamwork and sense of belonging they engender flourish at Dell "U" in the computer industry, at Motorola University in the cutting-edge field of semiconductors and electronics, at Thomson "U" in publishing, at Schwab University in financial services, and at Sears University in retailing. Countless others have teamed up with existing universities to custom-design programs and entire learning centres around the current and future needs of the company. Examples include Harley-Davidson working with Marquette University and Eaton's with Ryerson University.

2. **The Learning Budget**: At Cisco Systems Inc., the pre-eminent integrator of high-tech systems in America, employees receive an annual reimbursement of US$7,500 per year for tuition, provided they pass the course with a C grade or better. Meanwhile, Motorola, in addition to tuition reimbursement, commits to a minimum of 40 hours of training for each employee a year. Many others offer an exciting array of self-paced learning opportunities over the company's intranet.

   In a landmark study of job training and its link to employee turnover, the U.S. Bureau of Labor Statistics found that companies with high turnover provided only 7.2 hours of training per employee, compared with an average 10.7 hours per employee for all firms. Their study provided solid evidence that the higher the number of training hours offered, the lower the employee turnover rate.

3. **The Fastest Laptop**: Companies commit to providing their employees with the most modern technology available. Today's knowledge workers expect and take for granted acces to flat-screen monitors, the fastest hard drive, and the most sophisticated intranets.

4. **The Stock Purchase Plan**: Dell Computers call this its "Be Your Own Boss" program, which allows employees to purchase company shares at a 15 percent discount from what John Q. Public pays on the open market. Scores of companies allow their employees to buy company shares as of their *first* day on the job, an attractive perk for fast-growing companies with soaring stock prices.

5. **The Bonus Bonus**: Company bonuses are standard fare among high-knowledge industries. Here, pay for performance is the norm. Many take this notion one step further and give bonuses on top of individual performance bonuses when the company exceeds its growth and earnings targets for the year.

6. **Life-Cycle Assistance:** At Xerox, employees get to choose from a menu of benefits that they can customize to meet their specific needs. This represents a great step forward acknowledging diversity in the workplace at many of today's knowledge-based businesses. Some first-time home buyers choose mortgage assistance, or adoption assistance or child-care subsidies; those in the sandwich generation juggling the demands of teenagers and ageing parents simultaneously find the special TEENTALK assistance line and elder-care programs a godsend. Fidelity, the U.S. mutual fund giant, offers an amazing range of programs for working families, including back-up day care and vacation programs for school-age children.

177

7. **Cool Projects in a Neat Space:** A work-hard, play-hard philosophy has swept across today's workplace like a tidal wave. Bowling on Friday afternoons, pizza on Tuesdays, roller-blading tournaments in the parking lot, and jazzy on-site exercise facilities provide some stress relief for today's knowledge elite. But those companies that provide these knowledge workers with a continuous stream of cutting-edge projects that keeps them out in front of their industry peers deliver the real fun. For some of the best and brightest, learning has become a happy addiction in a New Economy in which people are paid to think, innovate, and define new frontiers continuously.

# New Rules — New Game

These coveted company assets can pick and choose among dozens of opportunities in today's job market. Their clout is already fuelling the growth of electronic commerce in the travel, florist, computer, automobile, and bookstore business, too. Single-handedly this group of workers is rewriting the rules of how our economy works. The U.S. Department of Commerce has published a landmark study on the emerging digital economy that antici-pates commerce on the Internet will surpass US$300 billion by the year 2002. General Electric, a world leader in e-commerce applications, predicts savings of US$500 million in slightly more than two years by purchasing US$5 billion in goods electronically.

High-knowledge industries in North America (those in which 40 percent of their employees are the knowledge workers defined in Chapter 1) employ almost *50* million people. To put the size of North America's elite workforce in perspective, consider that their numbers alone make them a market unto themselves nearly as large as the total population of France.

Comfortable with the latest technologies, they enjoy greater job security, higher incomes, and have the wherewithal to propel e-commerce into the next millennium.

Most marketers have yet to grasp the sheer size and force of this marketing bonanza nearly upon us. Direct-marketing organizations virtually ignore them, banks pay lip service to these clients with rudimentary Internet banking, and home builders do not recognize their phenomenal market potential. Think of the mass customization that would allow knowledge workers to configure the interior space of their homes — with furniture options — to suit their special needs and desires. Some hairstylists still offer old-fashioned mags to knowledge workers in search of new hairstyles in lieu of a computer database of styles and colours that the client can "try on" before the scissors ever begin to snip. Art galleries that fail to appreciate the online possibilities available to the artists they represent will find that those artists take their business elsewhere in the new economy. All businesses, the large and small alike, will be affected.

Not every company will embrace this giant market with gusto. Some among the established ranks of travel agencies, florists, and financial services see these changes as a dire threat to their profitability and market clout. To them, the knowledge era is alarming. In response, they seek to preserve their power by making themselves bigger and more powerful than the trends that threaten to engulf them and their businesses. They can't stop change. Others, like Amazon.com, Dell Computers, and Travelocity are trying to define and control the new terms of commerce by slashing established margins and doing business online.

Despite this, new ways of doing business and new ways of hiring and keeping employees content are the least of the challenges companies face. This transformation strikes to the very core of management principles and practices, and promises to revolutionize the world of finance as organizations attempt to safeguard their intellectual capital as people "go public."

# Lotka's Law

When A.J. Lotka published his groundbreaking if dull study on the frequency distribution of productivity in the June 1926 edition of the *Journal of the Washington Academy of Sciences*, he had little thought of sparking a revolution in the workplace less than a century later.

Along with the equally obscure work of Francis Galton, which estimated the rarity of outstanding men, Lotka's contribution provides the brilliant missing link in how to finance innovation — a vital link as the new knowledge economy emerges.

In a nutshell, their work revealed that a small number of highly innovative individuals lead the process of creativity within *any* organization. A 1995 study by Francis Narin and Anthony Breitzman, entitled "Inventive Productivity" and published in *Research Policy* (24), on the performance of highly productive scientists at four companies in the semiconductor industry confirmed just how relevant Lotka's Law had become today. In identifying key technological pacesetters Lotka stated that of every 100 scientists who produce one scientific paper each, 25 will produce two papers, 11 will produce three papers and so on, while only 1 scientist in the set will produce ten papers. The mathematics of innovation have a tremendous bearing on the knowledge economy because the differences between the rates of innovation and productivity in knowledge workers from the lowest to the highest producers are astoundingly large. A company that can identify and keep that one, single, most productive knowledge worker within its organization will have an enormous competitive edge in the marketplace.

# EBIT GODS OF THE TWENTY-FIRST CENTURY

The asset base of companies competing for growth in the knowledge economy will continue to shift more and more away from equipment, buildings, and other fixed assets to corporate knowledge assets. These assets exist in the form of creativity and intellectual capital, opening up an entirely new frontier. In this new world, knowledge workers become a source of capital themselves to the companies that employ them. They can become an enormous source of capital to themselves individually as well. This represents a seminal shift from labour as a cost of doing business to a new model in the knowledge economy in which these key workers can be quantified and securitized in their own right. In the past, would-be investors had the means to determine whether a company represented a solid investment and whether it was worth the value that it was trading at according to its *fixed* assets only.

Now knowledge-based companies can quantify their intellectual capital as well. By doing just that, they can issue a brand-new breed of derivative securities based on the track record of their key knowledge workers and their future value to the company's earnings before interest and taxes (EBIT for short).

Hockey teams, baseball, and basketball teams do this all the time as they trade the most talented players among themselves. But if 23-year-old hockey superstar Paul Kariya of the Mighty Ducks or Mark McGwire, who smashed baseball legend Roger Maris's home run record of 61 homers in a season, were listed on the stock exchange, why on earth would you not buy shares in them directly? Would you consider these immensely talented people any less desirable as investments than the company that makes the sports equipment they use?

Take it just one step further and you will see the investment possibilities a knowledge-based economy offers for North

America. Traditional global investment opportunities such as emerging market funds and Latin American funds are seen as riskier and risker because of the high levels of business corruption (see Chapter 2). In the years ahead, this continent's baby boom generation will move aggressively into its peak savings and investment years, so new investment vehicles will be required simply to absorb the large financial surpluses. The first country (hello, Canada!) to harness the full leverage of wealth creation successfully will enjoy an immeasurable lead.

Consider the following made-in-Canada example: Perhaps you already own shares in Sony Corp. of Japan, which is listed on the New York Stock Exchange, and have watched the value of those shares plummet to their current close of $79 ¼. You might have wished you'd had an opportunity to invest directly in recording superstar Céline Dion instead. Her forthcoming album from Sony Entertainment, *S'il suffisait d'aimer*, is scheduled to hit music stores in September 1998. Personally, I would pick Céline Inc. any day as an investment. I would prefer to base my retirement lifestyle on her natural talent and ability rather than on the ability of rigid "salarymen" within Tokyo's low-knowledge, high-corruption business circles to create wealth offshore.

This is where our economic future lies. We must be able to invest directly in the intellectual property and talent of Canada's first-class artists, athletes, writers, doctors, software developers, and engineers. Such investments would pave the way for these knowledge workers to raise immense pools of capital and leverage their knowledge bases into a long-term stream of earnings and dividends for all Canadians.

How differently our economic history could have unfolded. Consider the ramifications, had brilliant artists, actors, scientists, engineers, and others been able themselves to invest in a knowledge-based capital market, itself generated and compounded of the perpetual earnings based on such eminent people before them as Isaac Newton, William Shakespeare, or Wolfgang Amadeus Mozart. Accordingly, knowledge workers such as Alexander Graham Bell, Marie Curie, Elvis Presley, and Albert Einstein in this century could have enjoyed the wherewithal to pursue their own extraordinary talents to their very fullest, secure from financial worries, with access to such investment!

Such are the economics of the next century.

# 8

# THE NEXT CHAPTER
# IN CIVILIZATION

What differentiates a *new economy* from an entirely *new chapter in civilization and development*? Is it the magnitude of economic change? The wealth a nation is capable of creating or amassing? Is it the strength of its military? The number of patents a nation's scientists and innovators can file? Is it where we work, how we work, or what we work at?

History whispers otherwise.

The emergence of a new society capable of influencing and leading a new chapter in civilization requires more than mere technological prowess or the flexibility to adapt to new business opportunities.

Classical Greece, the Roman Empire, the European Renaissance — all marked major turning points in the advancement of humankind. None of them could be described as New Economies alone.

So how can we determine from our vantage point in history

whether the changes our generation has been through and the ones that lie ahead constitute another economic model in a long, albeit exciting, history of global change — or whether we stand at the brink of a whole new chapter in human development?

# ENDURING LEGACIES

Drive through any suburb in Canada and you will find here and there imposing columns gracing the homes of middle-class Canadians. Classically Greek in style, the columns are distinctly reminiscent of the Parthenon at the Acropolis or the graceful temple of Poseidon. The Greek view of life still enchants and excites us.

From the fine galleries in Atlantic Canada to the artist colonies that dot the west coast of Vancouver Island at Tofino and Uclulet, the sculpture of Canadian artists is still judged against the standards of the haunting grace of Venus de Milo, or the Discus Thrower, which masterfully portrayed the power and fine detail of the human body. Greek ideas on medicine and astronomy that date from before Christ were accepted with unquestioned faith until the 17th century when a new spirit of scientific experimentation emerged. To this day the Hippocratic oath is the standard to which Canada holds its doctors accountable.

The influence and ideals articulated by Pericles, the father of modern democracy, remain deeply entrenched in our understanding of the role and purpose of government. The unshakable belief in the worth of the individual citizen that formed the basis of Greek government and civilization has become the foundation of Canada's Charter of Rights and Freedoms 20 centuries later.

Ancient Greece has held a special place in the imagination for centuries. We see its legacy in our architecture, in our fine art collections, in our medicine, astronomy, in our laws, our philosophy and system of government and in many areas of modern thought.

Ancient Greece encompassed an area smaller than New Brunswick, and had only a few million inhabitants, but its influence on Western civilization extended far beyond its borders and its time. Population does not count when it comes to the ability of a nation to influence the course of civilization for centuries.

Other equally great epochs are indelibly inscribed on our culture, and are woven permanently into the fabric of our lives: municipal and provincial forms of government date from Roman times; so does the ritual of the three-course dinner, and the wedding ring. We acknowledge Roman architectural and engineering genius in the graceful arches of our bridges and the sports we watch in our modern coliseums and stadiums.

From Rome's mighty empire, Canada derives its strong sense of law and order. Cicero, Terence, Virgil, and Horace bequeathed us a legacy as some of the world's greatest thinkers. We hear their words, and those of other giants of Roman letters, in our daily lives:

> "Not worth his salt." — *Petronius*
> "While there's life, there's hope." — *Terence*
> "No sooner said than done." — *Ennius*
> "More brawn than brain." — *Nepos*
> "Love conquers all." — *Virgil*

Did either the Greeks or the Romans appreciate the extent of their impact on their worlds? By all accounts they did. "Future ages will wonder at us, as the present age wonders at us now," believed Pericles, the Greek statesman, orator, and general. The glory of Rome, too, was instilled in its citizens from birth. But the high esteem in which these people held their influence was not in the least capricious. Roman citizens believed in their nation's destiny and their *duty* to set the highest standards. They measured success by the greatness of the individual and his contribution to the breadth of his achievement.

Similarly, the emergence of Europe from the barbarian invasions and the Middle Ages that destroyed or drove underground much of the world's learning to date also marked far more than the growing pains of a New Economy. Like the Greeks and Romans who changed the course of civilization, the citizens of Florence, a city no more populous than North Bay, prided themselves on being sober men, devoted to their families and businesses and were deeply committed to being of service to their communities. (Debauchery and corruption came later.)

The good citizens of Florence built a city of such magnificence and beauty that it fostered an entire movement of genius in the arts, literature, and science. We still marvel at the splendour of the Renaissance. Works such as Dante's *Divine Comedy* and Machiavelli's *The Prince* and the creations of Michelangelo, Donatello, Raphael, Titian, Fra Angelico, and Giotto have left us their lasting legacy.

This rich era of European rebirth also furnished humankind with many of today's standard business practices: double-entry bookkeeping, holding companies, business-partnership agreements. Lawyers played a central role in their burgeoning New Economy. Through their daily practice of drafting agreements to keep up with the dramatic growth of trade and commerce, these practitioners recognized the need for an education very different from and more broadly based than that of the Middle Ages, which had emphasized religious studies. This profession was among the first to delve deeply into the legal legacy of its ancient Greek and Roman predecessors. From this renewed interest evolved a dramatically new focus on what we call the humanities, presented today as courses in history, literature, art, and music.

# Moving into the Next Century

Canada can foster a *New Economy*, as we have already done. We can and should take pride in this achievement, which Japan, Germany, France, and many others envy. But we can go further. We can use our national wealth and know-how to create a new vision and write the next chapter in the advance of Western civilization.

Wealth without vision is of little lasting consequence. The globe is littered with once prosperous cities and states that created vast wealth in their time, but little else. Bruges, for example, a picturesque town in the north of Belgium, attracts thousands of tourists annually who are delighted to take a step back in history. In the fifteenth century, this pretty town known for its beautiful lace, its lovely canals, and its picturesque Grande Place represented a formidable economic force that rivalled Venice in wealth and commerce.

Now, Bruges amounts to little more than a footnote in history. As its harbour gradually silted over, and vigorous trade moved elsewhere, its city fathers seemed incapable of seeing beyond their beautiful statue, the Madonna of Bruges, which they had commissioned from their favourite Italian sculptor, Michelangelo. Unlike Canada, they never even attempted to respond to the demands of their changing economy. Their broader potential to influence the course of human development was left largely untapped.

Today's Sultan of Brunei rules the world's richest country. Yet he and his nation are unlikely to merit even the footnote in history that medieval Bruges does. Business success matters, but high ideals such as integrity and qualities such as economic flexibility and a compelling vision on a national scale matter more.

Scientists can file patents that go unnoticed in the annals of scientific inquiry. Universities can be staffed by once promising minds who fight tooth and nail for the right to teach the same entry-level courses year in and year out for decades, in the name of academic independence. Military might can vanish overnight, as Mikhail Gorbachev and the citizens of the former Soviet Union can attest.

So, what *does* matter in the sweep of history? How can we Canadians determine whether we have simply crossed the threshold of a new economic model or whether we ought to prepare for an entirely new era in human civilization? What factors will decide which nation or culture leads the vanguard into the new millennium?

Money cannot create culture. But it can purchase the works that culture creates. (While ample lip service is given in Canada to a knowledge-based economy, our cyberbarons seem more at ease naming stadiums after themselves and their companies than in creating new knowledge and culture.) High education standards encourage an appreciation of culture as well as the basis for creating it. Every great chapter in human development has relied upon a revolutionary new system of education to convey a particular body of knowledge of, and ultimately a completely new definition of, culture to its people. To that end, the Internet of the twenty-first century could go beyond being a platform for the exchange of information and electronic commerce. It could also contribute to the creation of a new culture capable of advancing humankind. It offers us the promise of free, lifelong learning as the key to this new information age. With the lowest Internet charges in the world, Canada is superbly placed — better than most other countries — to take full advantage of this embryonic technology.

Along with *education*, every new chapter in civilization is also distinguished by its respect for *diversity*. This appreciation of new ideas and new ways of doing things and perceiving the world around them distinguished the Greeks, the Romans, and later the Florentines from their contemporary counterparts and assured their economic superiority in their own eras. Today such

**189**

recognition translates into what we in Canada call multicultural-ism and, in modern terminology, a respect for diversity. While parents today worry about the content of Internet chat rooms, a brand new culture is forming within this country in real time, one that relies on widely differing opinions and fresh ideas from outside Canada's borders and experience to date. Our commit-ment to this diversity and our deep respect for differences among our own people are important strengths on which to build.

Another key factor that will distinguish the nation that seizes this moment is *organization*, which is based on a deep belief in the value of cooperation. Canadians already espouse this value in many of their institutions and in private life.

From the cradle of civilization in ancient Mesopotamia to the pharaohs of ancient Egypt and the Greeks, Romans, and Euro-peans of the Renaissance who came after them, specific kinds of organization have branded each civilization as unique, have made possible its ready adaptation to changes, economic and otherwise, through the amalgamation of new cultures and beliefs. Canada already leads in this regard through its participation in such a vari-ety of international organizations as the OECD, the International Monetary Fund, the G-7, United Nations and many others. Yet many of us are continually surprised to hear in what high esteem Canadian organizational talents are held around the world.

Another portent of success is an unshakable belief in *the rule of law*. Every influential civilization has shaped its underlying beliefs and values into a rule of law that defines its view of itself and its world and eventually sweeps that world. Think of Rome's faith in individual equality before the law, the United States's Constitution recognizing government of the people, for the people, by the people. These notions were considered radical when they were introduced.

Each fresh chapter in human civilization contributes its own revolutionary means of *mass communication* as well: the invention of writing in Babylonian times; the open debates of the Roman citizenry, in which ordinary people had the chance to express their point of view; Gutenberg's revolutionary printing press, which spread the influence of Europe's Renaissance and the Reformation. Today's Internet beckons to us to embrace a world of communication connecting billions of minds and thoughts, sharing opinions and knowledge on a scale never before contemplated.

Consider, too, the effects of *scientific inquiry* on the very bases of civilization through the ages. Achievements in mathematics and astronomy paved the way for exploration, which developed into greater trade; developments in the pursuit of the various branches of science, mathematics, and engineering expanded the scope of human knowledge and made new discoveries possible. Today's breakthroughs centre around genomics and the miracles of modern medicine. Today, one out of every two Americans will survive through age 74. Fifty years ago, only half could expect to live to age 67. Through improved understanding of the effects of nutrition and exercise, scientists continue to work towards identifying new genes and cures.

And finally, unlike a nation or people that succeeds in terms of a New Economy alone, each new chapter in human civilization is defined by its *literature and the arts*. These reflect the soul of that civilization. Today, multimedia gurus are considered "cool" because they delineate what we consider the cutting edge of our changing culture. They are accorded the respect that centuries ago was reserved for the most respected of artists and poets.

The ability of a people to create a broadly based and balanced set of achievements depends on its ability to *acknowledge many new endeavours simultaneously*. This is the critical factor that can make the difference between just a new kind of economy and something far greater and of lasting significance. The value that a nation's citizens place on the broadest range of accomplishments performed to the highest standards — in literature, art, philosophy, politics, law, medicine, science, architecture, the military, engineering — is what signals each new era in civilization, rather than simply a nation's success in mastering a New Economy.

So we come to the question that concerns us most directly, the one on which Canada's future depends: What breadth of achievement are Canadians willing to strive for and attain? How far are Canadians willing to go in striving to go beyond the fruits of economic success and create the vision for civilization in the coming century? Only with self-awareness and a spirit of human achievement can a nation hope to make its most important contributions on the larger stage of civilization. If we Canadians are content merely to follow the lead set by others, we will have to be grateful for the material wealth we achieve in the twenty-first century — and nothing more.

However, the popular media, and television ratings, suggest a deep and growing hunger in Canada for something more — the will to seize our moment in history.

The millions of Canadians who tuned into the CBC's round-the-clock coverage of the 1998 Winter Games at Nagano were rewarded by the thrill of seeing Canadian athletes achieve the highest of Olympian standards. Canadians were awarded more Olympic medals than the United States, Japan, France, Italy, Sweden, Finland, Switzerland and many of the great nations that dominate winter sports worldwide.

Those 15 medals, the highest number for Canada ever, and the achievement of our youth represent a small but important step in what could and should become the birth of Canada's self-awareness.

Canadians can dominate the New Economy. We have the knowledge workers, we have the social infrastructure, we have the potential education and the communications technology, and we have the broad bases of organizational innovation, flexibility, and transparency, and a strong culture of scientific, artistic, and literary achievements on which to build. Add to these the will to create a new and sweeping vision for this exciting new age, and Canada will lead the way into the next century and beyond.